Alaska's National Wildlife Refuges

By Bruce Woods

ABOUT THIS ISSUE:

Bruce Woods of the U.S. Fish and Wildlife Service (USFWS) wrote the text for this book. In his words: "Although I'm listed as the author of this volume, it's actually the work of many people. In researching the national wildlife refuge system in Alaska, I've been fortunate to be able to call upon the science and writings of countless USFWS employees (as well as many in the U.S. Geological Survey, National Parks, Forest Service, and Alaska Department of Fish and Game). These men and women are too numerous to list individually, but this volume would not have been possible without access to the products of the years they spent both studying the trust resources of Alaska's refuges and communicating the importance of that research and those resources to the public. Many of them will recognize the results of their work, and even occasionally their words, in the pages that follow. Special thanks go to USFWS 'mapmaker extraordinaire' John Brewer for work above and beyond the call of duty.

"I'm also in debt to the refuge staffers, biologists, and others, including the editors of *ALASKA GEOGRAPHIC*®, who have taken time to review material in this book. Any credit for the accuracy of the pages that follow belongs in large part to them. Any mistakes that remain are my responsibility alone."

COVER: *Moose inhabit most regions of Alaska, and studies show they can live to 27 years. Only bulls grow antlers. (Craig Brandt)*

PREVIOUS PAGE: *In Alaska's far north, the sun rises in spring and doesn't set until late summer. This time exposure shows the "midnight sun" dipping near the horizon at Camden Bay, 30 miles west of Kaktovik at the edge of the Arctic National Wildlife Refuge (NWR). (Tom Walker)*

FACING PAGE: *Fall colors brighten the landscape beside Tustumena Glacier in Kenai NWR. (Chlaus Lotscher)*

EDITOR
Penny Rennick

PRODUCTION DIRECTOR
Kathy Doogan

ASSOCIATE EDITOR
Susan Beeman

MARKETING DIRECTOR
Mark Weber

BOARD OF DIRECTORS
Kathy Doogan
Carol Gilbertson
Penny Rennick

Robert A. Henning, **PRESIDENT EMERITUS**

ISBN: 1-56661-062-1

PRICE TO NON-MEMBERS THIS ISSUE: $24.95

PRINTED IN U.S.A.

POSTMASTER
Send address changes to:

ALASKA GEOGRAPHIC®
P.O. Box 93370, Anchorage, AK 99509-3370

ALASKA GEOGRAPHIC® (ISSN 0361-1353) is published quarterly by The Alaska Geographic Society, 639 West International Airport Rd. #38, Anchorage, AK 99518. Periodicals postage paid at Anchorage, Alaska, and additional mailing offices. Copyright © 2003 The Alaska Geographic Society. All rights reserved. Registered trademark: Alaska Geographic, ISSN 0361-1353; key title Alaska Geographic. This issue published March 2003.

THE ALASKA GEOGRAPHIC SOCIETY is a non-profit, educational organization dedicated to improving geographic understanding of Alaska and the North, putting geography back in the classroom, and exploring new methods of teaching and learning.

MEMBERS RECEIVE ALASKA GEOGRAPHIC®, a high-quality, colorful quarterly that devotes each issue to monographic, in-depth coverage of a specific northern region or resource-oriented subject. Back issues are available (see page 96). Membership is $49 ($59 to non-U.S. addresses) per year. To order or request our free catalog of back issues, contact: The Alaska Geographic Society, P.O. Box 93370, Anchorage, AK 99509-3370; phone (907) 562-0164 or toll free (888) 255-6697, fax (907) 562-0479, e-mail: akgeo@akgeo.com. A complete list of our back issues, maps, and other products can also be found on our website at www.akgeo.com.

SUBMITTING PHOTOGRAPHS: Those interested in submitting photos for possible publication should write or refer to our website for a list of upcoming topics or other photo needs and a copy of our editorial guidelines. We cannot be responsible for unsolicited submissions. Please note that submissions must be accompanied by sufficient postage for return by priority mail plus delivery confirmation.

CHANGE OF ADDRESS: When you move, the post office may not automatically forward your *ALASKA GEOGRAPHIC*® issues. To ensure continuous service, please notify us at least six weeks before moving. Send your new address and membership number or a mailing label from a recent issue of *ALASKA GEOGRAPHIC*® to: Address Change, Alaska Geographic Society, P.O. Box 93370, Anchorage, AK 99509-3370.

If your issue is returned by the post office because it is undeliverable, we will contact you to ask if you wish to receive a replacement for a small fee (to cover extra postage costs for having the issue returned to us and reshipping it to you).

PRE-PRESS: Graphic Chromatics

PRINTING: Banta Publications Group / Hart Press

The Library of Congress has cataloged this serial publication as follows:
Alaska Geographic. v.1-
  [Anchorage, Alaska Geographic Society] 1972-
  v. ill. (part col.). 23 x 31 cm.
  Quarterly
  Official publication of The Alaska Geographic Society.
  Key title: Alaska Geographic, ISSN 0361-1353.

  1. Alaska—Description and travel—1959-
  —Periodicals. I. Alaska Geographic Society.
F901.A266 917.98'04'505 72-92087
Library of Congress 75[79112] MARC-S.

Contents

National Wildlife Refuges: An American Inheritance

The nation behaves well if it treats the natural resources as assets which it must turn over to the next generation increased and not impaired in value.
— Pres. Theodore Roosevelt

America's national wildlife refuges are a grand inheritance, a wealth that even the poorest of its people can bequeath to their children. All of these public lands have ecological, spiritual, financial, and cultural value, but nowhere are these treasures so great, and this inheritance so rich, as in the refuges of Alaska.

If wild places have been the force that tempered the American spirit, how much more so have they shaped the Alaska identity? Alaskans live in what's commonly called the last frontier, implying an edge beyond which all is wild, or the great land, with all of the implications of immensity the phrase invokes. In the eyes of many Americans, and in the secret imaginations of many Alaska residents, Alaskans come from the sourdoughs, men and women who could still live by rod and gun, could still make a home for

LEFT: *Blue phase arctic fox kits nuzzle at the entrance to their den. This species is found along the Arctic Ocean and Bering Sea coasts as far south as the Aleutian Islands. (Loren Taft)*

FACING PAGE: *Guests of southwestern Alaska's Crystal Creek Lodge fly-fish on the Negukthlik River in Togiak NWR. Salmon, rainbow trout, arctic char, and grayling spawn in the region. (Fred Hirschmann)*

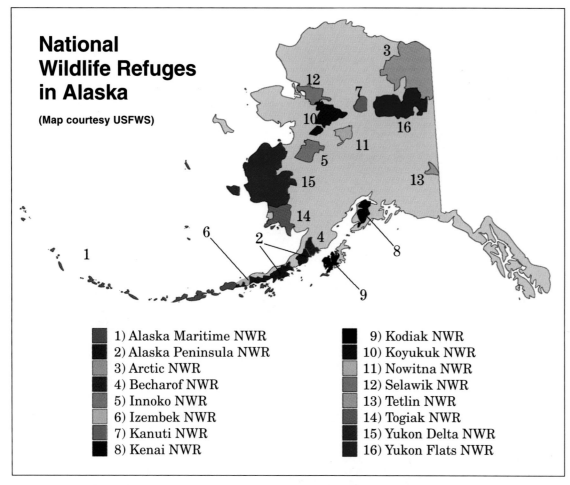

National Wildlife Refuges in Alaska

(Map courtesy USFWS)

1) Alaska Maritime NWR
2) Alaska Peninsula NWR
3) Arctic NWR
4) Becharof NWR
5) Innoko NWR
6) Izembek NWR
7) Kanuti NWR
8) Kenai NWR

9) Kodiak NWR
10) Koyukuk NWR
11) Nowitna NWR
12) Selawik NWR
13) Tetlin NWR
14) Togiak NWR
15) Yukon Delta NWR
16) Yukon Flats NWR

themselves in uncharted wilderness.

Many treasure the chance to be alone, to walk unaccompanied, or perhaps with a select few friends, into the nondenominational cathedrals of the wild. Even in Alaska, the world can sometimes become too much. The balm of wilderness does much to heal the sores of life in these early days of the twenty-first century.

When people venture into the "back of beyond" they are, regardless of the tents

and tools they take with them, stripping themselves of some of civilization's veneer. They become creatures that share the world again, connected to berries and bears, salmon and caribou, in a visceral way that, at the best of times, reminds them they are real. National wildlife refuges are a guarantee to the nation's children, to its grandchildren, that this universal tonic of wildness will be available to them, that they will have

the opportunity to feel alone under an endless sky, to move among the animals, to be healed.

Even seen only through the narrow lens of practicality, Alaska's refuges are rich. Waters of the Bristol Bay and Kodiak ecosystems, most of which are found on the Kodiak, Alaska Peninsula, and Becharof NWRs, are nurseries for annual commercial salmon catches that often exceed 100 million fish, and this fishery represents approximately half of the total U.S. annual harvest of wild salmon. Public hunting and fishing are available, even specified as "designated uses," on all of Alaska's refuges, bringing many thousands of dollars of license and equipment sales into state and local coffers and supporting a statewide guide/ outfitter industry. Add to that the tourist dollars the refuge system generates, in terms of actual visitation and in terms of the image of wildness Alaska's refuges project, and a bounty of practical wealth emerges. Kenai NWR hosts half a million visitors a year, and cruise ships sell the wonders of the state's coastal refuge lands. In fact, Alaska's refuges are a valuable component of the state's economy, one that, with proper care, is renewable and will provide income for generations of Alaskans to come.

Alaska's refuges are also sources of cultural wealth. Unlike other public lands in the United States, Alaska's refuges provide the opportunity for continued subsistence uses by local residents. What greater inheritance could there be than this, which allows Alaskans of many cultures to pass along skills necessary to live on the land, and the self-respect and reverence for the earth that such traditional knowledge often carries with it, to a new generation?

The word "refuge" is most simply defined as a place protected, and sometimes a place to flee to for comfort or safety. Alaska's national wildlife refuges are all that and more. They are preserves that protect the state's inheritances. They are places where plants and wildlife can continue their ancient dances, and thus provide people with not only an unsullied control against which to measure the man-made world, but also with the opportunity to reenter the pure natural world themselves and perhaps recover things they were not even aware they had lost. The refuges belong to every Alaskan, to every American. They are, quite simply, places of refuge for all. ■

Alaska's state flower, the forget-me-not, thrives in many northern regions. The arctic variety, shown here in the Pribilof Islands, part of Alaska Maritime NWR, grows to four inches. (Loren Taft)

More Than a Century of Conservation?

An unidentified woman models a hat decorated with feathers. In the late nineteenth and early twentieth centuries, many wading bird species were hunted to near extinction for their feathers, used on hats and accessories. Concerned people lobbied in support of the birds, starting a trend in species and habitat conservation that continues today. (National Archives and Records Administration, courtesy USFWS)

History can be slippery.

The official date for the centennial of the national wildlife refuge system is March 14, 2003. This date was chosen because it marks the 100th anniversary of the designation of Florida's Pelican Island as a federal bird sanctuary. The Pelican Island tale is certainly dramatic enough to inspire a centennial. It has a host of classic elements, including greed, a resource in danger, concerned and even heroic private citizens, and an inspired act by a charismatic leader.

It started with fashion. In the second half of the nineteenth century, feathered hats were a national millinery craze. Stylish women wore hats decorated with plumes, wings, sometimes entire stuffed birds, the more exotic the better. The fashion industry's hunger for feathers created an opportunity for market hunters, many of whom turned their attention from slaughtering waterfowl and upland game birds to supply trendy restaurants in the urban Northeast, to killing herons, egrets, spoonbills, and pelicans, among other species, to procure dramatic plumes for eager hat makers.

So successful were these market hunters that their depredations began to attract public attention. At the end of the 1850s, amateur naturalist Dr. Henry Bryant reported seeing thousands of herons, egrets, spoonbills, and pelicans nesting in the treetops of a tiny, three-acre island in Florida's Indian River Lagoon. The same observer also reported that plume hunters were shooting as many as 60 spoonbills a day. The productive rookeries of Pelican Island were in danger of being wiped out.

Help arrived in 1881 in the form of a German immigrant named Paul Kreugel, who homesteaded on Barker's Bluff, overlooking the lagoon. Kreugel drew attention to the plight of the birds being slaughtered on his doorstep and invited some of the United States's top naturalists to the area. Perhaps most influential of these guests was Frank Chapman, curator of the American Museum of Natural History. Discovering that Pelican Island was the sole active brown pelican rookery on the east coast of Florida, Chapman dedicated himself to its protection.

A conservation wind was blowing across the nation then, and Pelican Island's protectors soon had tools with which to

Chlaus Lotscher of Homer pauses above Green Lake, six miles east of Tustumena Lake in Kenai NWR. Dwarf birch (red) and willow (yellow) are among the first subalpine plants to turn color each fall. (Chlaus Lotscher)

work. The first was provided by the passage, in 1900, of the Lacey Act, a federal law prohibiting interstate commerce in illegally killed birds and other wildlife. This was followed, in Florida, by a state law, championed by the Florida Audubon Society and the American Ornithologists Union, prohibiting the killing of nongame bird species. To enforce these laws on Pelican Island, Kreugel was given a job as an "Audubon Warden" in 1902 and charged with guarding the island's birds.

But more powerful protectors were stirring. Chapman had managed to get the ear of Pres. Theodore Roosevelt, an amateur naturalist. On March 14, 1903, Roosevelt posed a simple question to his aides.

"Is there anything," he asked, "that prevents me from designating Pelican Island a federal bird sanctuary?" When the answer came back negative, T.R.'s reply was succinct. "Very well then. I so declare it." And that, many claim, was the beginning of the national wildlife refuge system.

As is often the case, however, Alaskans don't necessarily agree with the rest of the country. Alaskans have a tale of their own.

Their story starts with the founding of the U.S. Commission of Fish and Fisheries in 1871. Many, at that time, feared that

New England's coastal fisheries were in trouble. Spencer Baird, assistant secretary of the Smithsonian Institution and head of the National Museum, saw this as a time when science could be called on to protect these valuable national resources. He convinced Congress to establish the commission, commonly called the "Fish Commission," with himself serving as commissioner, though without salary. Baird set three broad goals for the new organization: to conduct a thorough study of the state of U.S. waters and the fish within them; to evaluate current and former commercial fishing methods and the collection of catch statistics; and to advance hatchery production, and the spread by introduction, of "useful food fishes."

Pres. Benjamin Harrison (below, left) authorized the establishment of Afognak Forest and Fish Culture Reservation on Afognak Island, part of the Kodiak archipelago, in 1892. In 1903 Pres. Theodore Roosevelt declared Florida's Pelican Island the first federal bird sanctuary. Historians differ on which proclamation initiated the United States's national wildlife refuge system. (Courtesy Library of Congress and USFWS)

Most of the early efforts of the Fish Commission focused on the country's Atlantic fisheries. In comparison, commercial fishing on the Pacific Coast was still in its infancy. However, Atlantic salmon stocks were already depleted, and Baird thought he could see a solution in the West. Accordingly, he sent a fish culturist named Livingston Stone to California, where Stone and his associates, in just 15 days, built the nation's first federal fish hatchery on the banks of northern California's McCloud River. In those days there was none of the hesitancy about species introduction that, with a century of hindsight as guide, today's land

managers might feel. Soon king salmon eggs were being sent east; of the first 30,000 that were shipped, less than one percent eventually reached fingerling size. From that humble beginning, however, grew the federal fish hatchery system, which provides sport fish and supports the restoration of endangered species across the United States today.

Other than Stone's brave experiment though, the commission maintained a degree of eastern myopia until 1888. Then, under orders of Commissioner Marshall McDonald, who a few months after Baird's death in 1887 had become the first full-time, and full-salaried, commissioner, the Fish Commission's research vessel *Albatross* set out for a 26-year stint in Pacific waters, during which time she visited Alaska.

At the same time, Stone had become increasingly caught up in salmon culture. Although Pacific salmon stocks were still abundant, Stone's experiences and his knowledge of the history of Atlantic salmon made him fear for the future of this seemingly inexhaustible resource.

Playing the role Chapman would play in Florida more than a decade later, Stone captured the ears of the powerful and lobbied for creation of a "National Salmon Park" in Alaska, to guarantee that the chinook, sockeye, coho, pink, and chum of the Pacific would never go the way of the passenger pigeon.

Acting upon Stone's vision in 1892, 11 years before Roosevelt asked his simple question about Pelican Island, an equally visionary, if perhaps less charismatic, Pres. Benjamin Harrison proclaimed the establishment of the Afognak Forest and

An ANILCA Primer

Public Law 96-487, the 1980 Alaska National Interest Lands Conservation Act (ANILCA), established more than 100 million acres of conservation lands in Alaska. These included wildlife refuges, national parks, national forests, and wild and scenic rivers. ANILCA added 54 million acres to the national wildlife refuge system in Alaska, creating nine new refuges and expanding and/or renaming seven already established units.

The origins of ANILCA date back to 1958. The Alaska Statehood Act, which transformed the Territory of Alaska into the 49th state, authorized Alaska officials to select for its economic basis 104 million acres from a total land area of 375 million acres, all of which was federal land. The march toward ANILCA continued with passage of the 1971 Alaska Native Claims Settlement Act (ANCSA), which recognized the rights of Alaska Natives by granting them the opportunity to select approximately 44 million acres of the remaining federal land in Alaska. A separate component of ANCSA, Section 17(d)(2), directed the secretary of the interior to make a large withdrawal of public lands suitable for addition to existing, or creation of new, conservation units within the state.

In announcing the government's recommendations for these withdrawals in 1977, Secretary of the Interior Cecil D. Andrus made the following statement: "Through enactment of our proposals, we can be certain that the crown jewels of Alaska — its most spectacular natural environments,

recreation areas, and wildlife habitats — will remain in trust for the benefit of our nation's citizens.

"When we talk of conserving resources for our nation and for the future, we must put this in perspective. It is not our intention to 'lock up' the State of Alaska, and our plan provides sufficient latitude for needed development."

The conservation unit lands established under ANILCA are unique in the country; they include provisions that allow local people to pursue traditional activities and lifestyles, including subsistence hunting and fishing, on the selected lands.

No state or private lands were withdrawn to create national wildlife refuges under ANILCA. Instead, select federal lands that were previously under supervision of the Bureau of Land Management or the U.S. Forest Service and were judged to have high wildlife values were transferred to USFWS to be managed as refuges. ■

Years of intense public and congressional debate preceded Pres. Jimmy Carter signing ANILCA, which created millions of acres of conservation lands, into law in 1980. Here, President Carter tries his luck fishing in Alaska waters. (Courtesy Jimmy Carter Library)

Fish Culture Reservation on Afognak Island in Alaska. Interestingly, the law Harrison used to create the Afognak "refuge," the Forest Reserve Act of 1891, was itself the result of lobbying by a number of concerned individuals, several of whom had organized in 1887 to form the Boone and Crockett Club, under the leadership of none other than Theodore Roosevelt.

Harrison's proclamation created, some Alaska contrarians would argue, the first unit in the national wildlife refuge system, and portions of the area thus protected remain part of the Kodiak and Alaska Maritime NWRs.

But whether the national wildlife refuge system began on Pelican Island or Afognak, some of the defining moments of its future would, unarguably, take place in Alaska. ■

Dave Spencer, Alaska Refuge Pioneer

Although he once downplayed the significance of his career with USFWS by saying, "I was a wandering duck counter," Dave Spencer was instrumental in shepherding Kenai NWR and the national wildlife refuge system in Alaska through some of its greatest challenges. Spencer brought a double-barreled background with him when he arrived in Alaska in 1948. He knew airplanes, having served as a flight instructor in World War II, and he knew conservation as a result of his postmilitary graduate school work with legendary environmentalist Aldo Leopold.

After leaving college, Spencer spent several years working for USFWS in the Lower 48, flying waterfowl surveys from Guatemala to northern Saskatchewan. He came to Alaska to serve as the first manager of the Kenai National Moose Range, which had been established just days after the United States entered World War II.

Refuge life in Alaska, even on such a "settled" refuge as Kenai, wasn't exactly posh in the middle of the last century.

"We had to ship our car on the train to Moose Pass," Spencer remembered during a late 1990s interview. "Fish and Wildlife had a plane and the pilot said he'd run me down to the house. It was a pretty good-looking house, not very fancy. No plumbing, no water, had a pump in the kitchen like you see in campgrounds today."

Spencer managed Kenai National Moose Range for two years. During that time he presided over the first attempts to determine baseline populations for moose and other wildlife on the range.

"To manage moose," he said, "you need to

know how many you have. So you design a sampling plan and go fly the survey. But first you go out in the dark winter morning and drape tarps over both engines of your Grumman Widgeon. Get a couple of plumber's firepots going and carefully arrange them under the tarps. Watch for a couple hours so the engines warm up without torching the whole plane. Roar off into the rising sun and fly for several hours, recording numbers and locations of moose. Land at dark and tie down the plane with frozen ropes. After supper, take over

the kitchen table and calculate the statistics on a hand-cranked adding machine."

In 1950 Spencer was promoted to regional refuge supervisor, overseeing all refuge lands in Alaska, a job he held until his retirement in 1976. He fought for and guided the refuge system in Alaska through the turbulent years of poachers and squatters, oil development, statehood, emerging wilderness and environmental ethics, and supported ANILCA. Such were his contributions to USFWS in Alaska that, in 1997, USFWS's Alaska Regional Director Dave Allen signed a Record of Decision renaming the Canoe Lakes Unit of the Kenai Wilderness as the Dave Spencer Wilderness. In so doing, Allen recognized Spencer as the "individual most responsible for guiding the establishment of the national wildlife refuge system in Alaska as a diverse collection of dynamic ecosystems set aside to conserve lasting habitat for wildlife and to provide continued opportunities for traditional and compatible uses for people who treasure these wildlands."

Dave Spencer passed away on February 9, 2000. The lands named after him, and, more importantly, the memories of the many USFWS employees who worked with and admired him, serve as a memorial for a simple "wandering duck counter." ∎

Dave Spencer, regional refuge supervisor in Alaska from 1950 to 1976, captures an Aleutian Canada gosling on Buldir Island, in the western Aleutians, for banding and measuring. (Jim Bartonek, courtesy USFWS)

Evolution of the National Wildlife Refuge System in Alaska

CONSERVATION UNIT NAME	PROCLAIMING DOCUMENT	DATE	ACTION BY	REASON FOR ACTION	GEOGRAPHIC AREA
Afognak Forest and Fish Culture Reservation	Proclamation 39	12/24/1892	Pres. Benjamin Harrison	"in order that salmon fisheries in the water of the Island, and salmon and other fish and sea animals, and other animals and birds, and the timber, undergrowth, grass, moss, and other growth in, on, and about said Island may be protected and preserved unimpaired, and it appears that the public good would be promoted by setting apart and reserving said lands as a public reservation."	Afognak Island, Sealion Rocks, Sea Otter Island, and water surrounding Afognak Island
Bering Sea Reservation	Executive Order 1037	2/27/1909	Pres. Theodore Roosevelt	"are hereby reserved and set apart for the use of the Department of Agriculture as a preserve and breeding ground for native birds."	St. Matthew Island
Tuxedni Reservation	Executive Order 1039	2/27/1909	Pres. Theodore Roosevelt	"are hereby reserved and set apart for the use of the Department of Agriculture as a preserve and breeding ground for native birds."	Chisik and Duck Islands
Saint Lazaria Reservation	Executive Order 1040	2/27/1909	Pres. Theodore Roosevelt	"is hereby reserved and set apart for the use of the Department of Agriculture as a preserve and breeding ground for native birds."	St. Lazaria Island
Yukon Delta Reservation	Executive Order 1041	2/27/1909	Pres. Theodore Roosevelt	"is hereby reserved and set apart for the use of the Department of Agriculture as a preserve and breeding ground for native birds."	Yukon Delta area
Bogoslof Reservation	Executive Order 1049	2/27/1909	Pres. Theodore Roosevelt	"are hereby reserved and set apart for the use of the Department of Agriculture as a preserve and breeding ground for native birds."	Bogoslof Islands
Forrester Island Reservation	Executive Order 1458	1/11/1912	Pres. William H. Taft	"are hereby reserved and set apart for the use of the Department of Agriculture as a preserve and breeding ground for native birds."	Forrester Island and Wolf Rock
Hazy Islands Reservation	Executive Order 1459	1/11/1912	Pres. William H. Taft	"are hereby reserved and set apart for the use of the Department of Agriculture as a preserve and breeding ground for native birds."	Hazy Islands

CONSERVATION UNIT NAME	PROCLAIMING DOCUMENT	DATE	ACTION BY	REASON FOR ACTION	GEOGRAPHIC AREA
Chamisso Island Reservation	Executive Order 1658	12/7/1912	Pres. William H. Taft	"are hereby reserved and set apart for the use of the Department of Agriculture as a preserve and breeding ground for native birds."	Chamisso Island
Aleutian Islands Reservation	Executive Order 1733	3/3/1913	Pres. William H. Taft	"are hereby reserved and set apart as a preserve and breeding ground for native birds, for the propagation of reindeer and fur bearing animals, and for the encouragement and development of the fisheries. Jurisdiction over the wild birds is hereby placed with the Department of Agriculture, and jurisdiction over the fisheries, seal, sea otter, cetaceans and other aquatic species, is placed with the Department of Commerce and Labor."	Unimak Island and Sanak Islands west to Attu Island
Yukon Delta Reservation revoked	Executive Order 3642	2/27/1922	Pres. Warren G. Harding	"reserving and setting aside for the use of the Department of Agriculture as a preserve and breeding ground for native birds the treeless tundra of the delta of the Yukon River."	Yukon Delta area
Aleutian Islands Reservation revoked in part	Executive Order 5000	11/23/1928	Pres. Calvin Coolidge	"a preserve and breeding ground for native birds, for the propagation of reindeer and fur bearing animals, and for the encouragement and development of the fisheries, be and it is hereby revoked in so far as it affects the following named islands – Akun, Akutan, Sanak, Tigalda, Umnak and Unalaska, including Sedanka."	Akun, Akutan, Sanak, Tigalda, Umnak, and Unalaska, including Sedanka, Islands
Nunivak Island Reservation	Executive Order 5095	4/15/1929	Pres. Herbert Hoover	"set apart for the use of the Department of Agriculture [for] conducting experiments in the crossing and propagation of reindeer and native caribou, for contemplated experiments in reestablishing the musk ox as a native animal of Alaska, and also as a preserve and breeding ground for native birds and wild game and fur bearing animals."	Nunivak Island
Aleutian Islands Reservation reduced	Executive Order 5243	12/19/1929	Pres. Herbert Hoover	"a preserve and breeding ground for native birds, for the propagation of reindeer and fur bearing animals, and for the encouragement and development of the fisheries, be and it is hereby revoked in so far as it affects all of Amaknak Island."	Amaknak Island

CONSERVATION UNIT NAME	PROCLAIMING DOCUMENT	DATE	ACTION BY	REASON FOR ACTION	GEOGRAPHIC AREA
Aleutian Islands Reservation enlarged	Executive Order 5318	4/7/1930	Pres. Herbert Hoover	"are hereby reserved and set apart for the use of the Department of Agriculture as a refuge and breeding ground for native birds and wild animals."	Amak Island
Nunivak Island Reservation enlarged	Executive Order 5470	10/22/1930	Pres. Herbert Hoover	"are hereby reserved and set apart for the use of the Department of Agriculture as a refuge and breeding ground for native birds and game and furbearing animals."	Nunivak and Triangle Islands and submerged land
Semidi Islands Wildlife Refuge	Executive Order 5858	6/17/1932	Pres. Herbert Hoover	"are hereby reserved from all forms of appropriation under the public land laws and set apart for the use of the Department of Agriculture as a refuge and breeding ground for wild birds and game and fur animals."	Semidi Islands and submerged lands.
Hazen Bay Migratory Waterfowl Refuge	Executive Order 7770	12/14/1937	Pres. Franklin D. Roosevelt	"reserved and set apart, subject to valid existing rights, for the use of the Department of Agriculture as a refuge and breeding ground for migratory birds and other wildlife."	Nunivachak and Kigigak Islands
Changing names of certain federal wildlife refuges	Proclamation 2416	7/27/1940	Pres. Franklin D. Roosevelt	Aleutian Islands Reservation to Aleutian Islands National Wildlife Refuge; Bering Sea Reservation to Bering Sea National Wildlife Refuge; Bogoslof Reservation to Bogoslof National Wildlife Refuge; Chamisso Island Reservation to Chamisso National Wildlife Refuge; Forrester Island Reservation to Forrester Island National Wildlife Refuge; Hazen Bay Migratory Waterfowl Refuge to Hazen Bay National Wildlife Refuge; Hazy Islands Reservation to Hazy Islands National Wildlife Refuge; Nunivak Island Reservation to Nunivak National Wildlife Refuge; Saint Lazaria Reservation to Saint Lazaria National Wildlife Refuge; Semidi Islands Wild Life Refuge to Semidi National Wildlife Refuge; Tuxedni Reservation to Tuxedni National Wildlife Refuge.	various
Kodiak National Wildlife Refuge	Executive Order 8857	8/19/1941	Pres. Franklin D. Roosevelt	"withdrawn and reserved for the use of the Department of the Interior and the Alaska Game Commission as a refuge and breeding ground for brown bears and other wildlife."	Kodiak and Uganik Islands

CONSERVATION UNIT NAME	PROCLAIMING DOCUMENT	DATE	ACTION BY	REASON FOR ACTION	GEOGRAPHIC AREA
Kenai National Moose Range	Executive Order 8979	12/16/1941	Pres. Franklin D. Roosevelt	"withdrawn and reserved for the use of the Department of the Interior and the Alaska Game Commission as a refuge and breeding ground for moose."	Kenai Peninsula
Simeonof National Wildlife Refuge	Public Land Order 1749	10/30/1958	Fred A. Seaton (secretary of interior)	"reserved and set apart for the use of the United States Fish and Wildlife Service, Department of Interior, as a refuge for the preservation and propagation of the sea otter and other wildlife thereon."	Simeonof Island and one mile buffer of sub-merged lands
Kuskokwim National Wildlife Range	Public Land Order 2213	12/6/1960	Fred A. Seaton	"reserved for the use of the Department of the Interior as a refuge, breeding grounds and management area for all forms of wildlife."	North and south of Nelson Island near Baird Inlet
Arctic National Wildlife Range	Public Land Order 2214	12/6/1960	Fred A. Seaton	"purpose of preserving unique wildlife, wilderness and recreational values."	Northeastern Alaska
Izembek National Wildlife Range	Public Land Order 2216	12/6/1960	Fred A. Seaton	"reserved for the use of the Department of the Interior as a refuge, breeding grounds and management area for all forms of wildlife."	Cold Bay area
Kuskokwim National Wildlife Range renamed	Public Land Order 2253	1/16/1961	Fred A. Seaton	Kuskokwim National Wildlife Range to Clarence Rhode National Wildlife Range.	North and south of Nelson Island near Baird Inlet
Cape Newenham National Wildlife Refuge	Public Land Order 4583	1/20/1969	Stewart L. Udall (secretary of interior)	"areas possess outstanding wildlife values, including possibly the greatest bird colony on the North American Continent and important habitat for other terrestrial and marine wildlife ... and reserved for the protection of wildlife and their habitat."	Cape Newenham and Cape Peirce area
Additions to Clarence Rhode National Wildlife Range	Public Land Order 4584	1/20/1969	Stewart L. Udall	"purpose of preserving the said waterfowl and other wildlife values and the habitat."	Mouth of Yukon River, part of Nelson Island, and area just west of Hooper Bay

CONSERVATION UNIT NAME	PROCLAIMING DOCUMENT	DATE	ACTION BY	REASON FOR ACTION	GEOGRAPHIC AREA
Alaska National Interest Lands Conservation Act (ANILCA)	Public Law 96-487	12/2/1980	Pres. Jimmy Carter	"In order to preserve for the benefit, use, education, and inspiration of present and future generations certain lands and waters in the State of Alaska that contain nationally significant natural, scenic, historic, archeological, geological, scientific, wilderness, cultural, recreational, and wildlife values."	various
				Created: Alaska Peninsula National Wildlife Refuge, Becharof National Wildlife Refuge, Innoko National Wildlife Refuge, Kanuti National Wildlife Refuge, Koyukuk National Wildlife Refuge, Nowitna National Wildlife Refuge, Selawik National Wildlife Refuge, Tetlin National Wildlife Refuge, Yukon Flats National Wildlife Refuge.	various
				Renamed: Izembek National Wildlife Range to Izembek National Wildlife Refuge.	Cold Bay area
				Enlarged: Alaska Maritime National Wildlife Refuge – Additional land plus Aleutian Islands National Wildlife Refuge, Bering Sea National Wildlife Refuge, Bogoslof National Wildlife Refuge, Chamisso National Wildlife Refuge, Forrester Island National Wildlife Refuge, Hazy Islands National Wildlife Refuge, Saint Lazaria National Wildlife Refuge, Semidi National Wildlife Refuge, Simeonof National Wildlife Refuge, and Tuxedni National Wildlife Refuge; Arctic National Wildlife Refuge – Additional land plus Arctic National Wildlife Range; Kenai National Wildlife Refuge – Additional land plus Kenai National Moose Range; Kodiak National Wildlife Refuge – Additional land plus Kodiak National Wildlife Refuge; Togiak National Wildlife Refuge – Additional land plus Cape Newenham National Wildlife Refuge; Yukon Delta National Wildlife Refuge – Additional land plus Hazen Bay National Wildlife Refuge, Nunivak National Wildlife Refuge, and Clarence Rhode National Wildlife Range.	various

Alaska's National Wildlife Refuges

Alaska Maritime NWR

Alaska Maritime NWR encompasses great distances and greater dramas. Here winds whip through the grasses of rugged, wave-pounded islands and active volcanoes simmer, venting steam above collars of fog. It is a place of contrasts, where relics of a past war slowly rust in deserted valleys while nearby, great forests of kelp teem with life. It is, and has long been, a place of refuge, and has seen some of the most dramatic wildlife conservation stories in the nation's history.

Containing some of the first conservation units to be established in the United States, today's Alaska Maritime NWR includes lands that were formerly parts of Aleutian Islands, Bering Sea, Bogoslof, Chamisso, Forrester Island, Hazy Islands, St. Lazaria, Semidi, and Tuxedni NWRs. Ranging in size from the approximately 1.3-million-acre Aleutian Islands Wilderness to the 32-acre Hazy Islands Wilderness, many of these units are still represented among the 10 distinct congressionally designated Wilderness areas included in Alaska Maritime.

Because it is spread out along most of the thousands of miles of Alaska's coastline, the sheer span of this refuge is difficult to grasp. Its more than 2,500 islands, islets, spires, rocks, reefs, waters, and headlands extend from Forrester Island, in Southeast, to the westernmost tip of the Aleutians, and north to Cape Lisburne on the Arctic Ocean. Traveling

FACING PAGE: *Ushagat, largest of the Barren Islands, is part of Alaska Maritime NWR and lies at the mouth of Cook Inlet in Southcentral. (Fred Hirschmann)*

between its farthest-flung points would be the equivalent of taking a trip from Georgia to California.

No other maritime national wildlife refuge is as large or as productive. Alaska Maritime's coastal lands provide nesting habitat for approximately 40 million seabirds, about 80 percent of Alaska's nesting seabird population and more than half of the nesting seabirds in the United States. Many of these species nest in colonies on rocky islands or beach cliffs. A single such colony might be home to more than a million birds, and include as many as a dozen species.

As incredible as Alaska Maritime's seabird spectacle is, however, the refuge's total bird story is bigger still. Because its lands provide important resting and feeding stops for migrants from several continents, the refuge hosts an almost unimaginable variety of bird life. More than 250 species have been sighted on Alaska Maritime, some of which are rarely seen elsewhere in the United States. This fact has made the refuge, and in particular the Aleutian and Pribilof Islands, a coveted vacation spot for birders. For the considerable cost of a flight to Unalaska or St. Paul and the hire

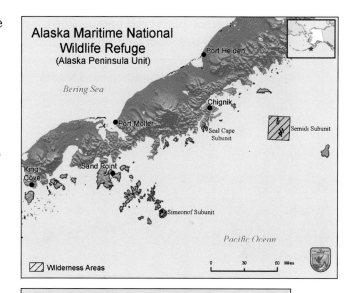

Alaska Maritime NWR

Established: Some areas first protected in 1892
Acreage: 3,435,246
Designated Wilderness: 2,576,320 acres
Location: All islands, islets, rocks, and spires along Alaska's coast from the Gulf of Alaska to the Bering and Chukchi Seas that are not otherwise designated or privately owned, as well as some headlands

of a bird-watching tour guide, even the most jaded of birders is likely to be able to add a species or two to his or her life list of birds identified.

Perhaps the most dramatic of Alaska Maritime's bird stories concerns the recovery of the Aleutian Canada goose. These geese nest only on a few islands in the Aleutians. Driven to presumed extinction by the introduction of non-native foxes to their breeding islands, the birds have since recovered and, in 2001, were removed from the Endangered

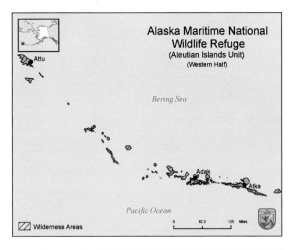

Sea Otters of the Aleutians

The northern sea otter (*Enhydra lutris kenyoni*) has endured a troubled history along the Aleutian archipelago during the past two centuries. This small marine mammal, largest member of the weasel family, has already recovered once from near-extermination, and is now in the middle of an unexplained population decline of similar severity.

Primarily creatures of coastal waters, sea otters can eat approximately a quarter of their body weight each day from a menu that consists mainly of slow-moving bivalves, crustaceans, and sea urchins. Despite their prodigious appetites, sea otters lack the layer of blubber that warms most marine mammals in the frigid waters of the Aleutians. Instead, these creatures rely on their fur for insulation. So dense are these protective coats that an adult sea otter can sport as many as 650,000 hairs per square inch of body area. It was this magnificent fur that lead to the otters' first near-extinction.

No one knows how many sea otters frolicked in Alaska waters before the 1741 Vitus Bering-Alexei Chirikof expedition alerted Russian fur hunters to

the wonders of sea otter pelts. It has been estimated, however, that in the 170 years of hunting that followed, a worldwide total of somewhere between 500,000 and a million sea otters were killed. In the closing days of the hunt, rarity had driven the price of a single sea otter pelt to nearly $1,000, making them the most valuable furs in history. When help finally arrived in the form of the Treaty for the Preservation and Protection of Fur Seals and Sea Otters in 1911, which provided complete protection from commercial harvest, only two isolated colonies of otters remained in the entire Aleutian archipelago, in the Rat and Delarof Islands. At the time, the total world population of northern sea otters was perhaps no greater than 1,000 animals.

Under protection, the Aleutian otters recovered, with remnant populations growing and gradually recolonizing their former range. The first systematic counts of sea otters in the Aleutian archipelago were conducted between 1957 and 1965 by USFWS biologist Karl W. Kenyon. Kenyon is widely recognized as the grandfather of sea otter research, hence the subspecies' name *kenyoni*. By the end of Kenyon's surveys, sea otters were thought to have reached optimum population levels on 23 islands in the western and central Aleutians. By the mid 1980s they had returned to every major island group in the archipelago. Though they had not yet reached estimated historical population levels prior to the fur trade,

Thick fur keeps this sea otter warm in Alaska's frigid waters. (Tom Walker)

St. Lazaria Islands, 15 miles southwest of Sitka, are included in Alaska Maritime NWR. Southeast Alaska is home to several marine mammal species, including sea otters. (Courtesy USFWS)

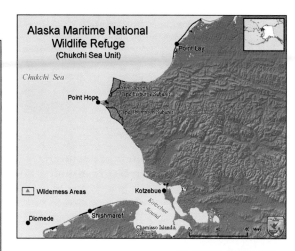

half of the world's sea otters, perhaps more than 70,000 animals, were found in the Aleutians. The future looked bright.

Then in 1992, USFWS conducted the first survey of the entire Aleutian sea otter population since Kenyon's groundbreaking work. Biologists were shocked to discover that populations had declined to half of those counted in 1965 in the western and central Aleutians. These were areas in which, only 27 years before, the otters had supposedly been thriving. In 2000 USFWS conducted a follow-up aerial survey and found that in the years since the 1992 survey, the sea otter population had declined again, in some areas by as much as 90 percent, and by 70 percent throughout the archipelago. Today's estimates tally as few as 9,000 otters in the Aleutians. The speed and severity of the population crash are clear; the reasons behind it are not.

Research to date seems to indicate that disease, starvation, and contaminants can be ruled out as major contributors to the current decline in the Aleutians. There is no commercial harvest and the Native subsistence kill is thought to be far too small to be a factor. One theory, proposed by biologists Jim Estes and Tim Tinker of the U.S. Geological Survey (USGS) Biological Resources Division, suggests that predation by orcas (killer whales) may be behind the decline. Though this is admittedly still a theory, and not without its detractors, it is supported by several

facts. First, there was a significant increase in the number of observed attacks by orcas on sea otters during the 1990s. Second, there has been no observed increase in otter carcasses washing ashore, which might be expected if something other than predation was the cause of decline. Finally, in at least one area otter populations have remained steady in a protected lagoon that killer whales cannot enter, while over the same period, otter numbers have declined by 70 percent in the adjacent exposed bay.

Additional surveys in 2001 and 2002 revealed that the sea otter decline is not limited to the Aleutian archipelago, but is widespread across southwestern Alaska; southeastern Alaska populations are either stable or growing. Currently, USFWS is preparing a proposed rule to explore the possibility of listing the sea otter in southwestern Alaska as threatened under the Endangered Species Act. Such a listing would focus additional resources on the population decline and improve chances that this marine mammal can climb back from the edge of extinction yet again. ■

Species Act's list of threatened species.

Besides foxes and other introduced animals such as caribou, reindeer, ground squirrels, and rats, the last of which still pose a threat to native birds, most of the refuge's lands, with the exception of mainland areas and islands near shore, are not home to land mammals. Marine mammals, however, are another story. Refuge lands and surrounding waters are critical to maintaining healthy populations of sea otters, Alaska's declining population of Steller sea lions, and

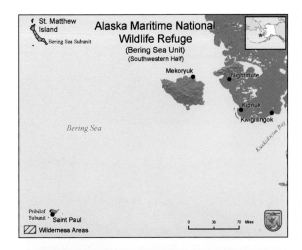

Known for his sea otter research, USFWS biologist Karl W. Kenyon, left, helps Ray Erickson feed Aleutian Canada geese in 1971. The birds were on their way to the Aleutian Islands as part of a species recovery program. (Rex Gary Schmidt, courtesy USFWS)

northern fur seals. In addition, polar bears and walrus are found on the northern units of the refuge, and at least seven species of whales and two of porpoise can

be found seasonally near refuge lands.

Portions of Alaska Maritime had been settled, prior to the eighteenth-century Russian voyages of discovery, by all of Alaska's coastal Native peoples, particularly the Aleuts, many of whom continue to pursue subsistence lifestyles on refuge lands and surrounding waters. More recent U.S. history was made in World War II, when the Japanese captured Kiska and Attu, the only U.S. lands occupied during that conflict, and, later, when the United States conducted atomic bomb tests on

Amchitka Island during the Cold War.

Though much of Alaska Maritime is extremely remote, some of its bird colonies are regularly visited by commercial sightseeing boats operating out of Seward, Sitka, and Homer. Charters can also be arranged out of other coastal communities located near refuge lands, including Kodiak, Nome, Unalaska, St. Paul, and Sand Point. Summer, when birds are nesting and sea lions and seals are pupping on the beaches, is the best time to visit, though cool temperatures, high winds, and precipitation can be expected on most refuge lands even then. One of the most interesting ways to experience the refuge is by traveling on the ferry from Homer to Kodiak or Unalaska during summer. Refuge naturalists accompany the boat, presenting wildlife programs and helping passengers identify birds and mammals seen along the way. ■

FACING PAGE: *Biologists count seabirds at Cape Thompson, on Alaska's Chukchi Sea coast, in July 1991. (David Roseneau)*

Bob "Sea Otter" Jones

A native of Milbank, South Dakota, Bob Jones attended South Dakota State College, where he earned a Bachelor of Science degree before moving north to earn his Master in biology from the University of Alaska Fairbanks. Alaska was to fascinate him for the rest of his career.

Jones first came to the Aleutians while serving as a radar officer in the U.S. Army during World War II. He moved to Kodiak after the war, but soon turned his attention to the Aleutian archipelago again, when, in 1948, he joined USFWS as manager of Aleutian Islands NWR. A skilled doryman, Jones visited the remote islands in his care, often landing on dangerous, surf-battered shorelines in one of these sturdy, little workhorse boats.

He earned his nickname in the early 1950s, when he was involved in attempts to return northern sea otters to their former Aleutian range. Though these early efforts were unsuccessful, Jones's work, coupled with that of other USFWS biologists, notably Karl W. Kenyon, eventually led to a strong recovery for the species.

Though the nickname "Sea Otter" was to prove permanent, one of the highlights of Jones's career involved another species in need of help: the Aleutian Canada goose. This small member of the brant family was another victim of the fur industry, though indirectly. In the mid 1700s, nonindigenous foxes were introduced onto islands in the Aleutian chain. The furbearers thrived on the remote islands, where they fed on seabirds and their eggs, and eventually supported a profitable fur trade. By 1936, foxes had been introduced to at least 190 islands in the Aleutians alone, and to more than 400 islands along Alaska's coast. These were all within the sole breeding range of the Aleutian Canada goose. The birds were particularly defenseless against foxes. They are ground nesters, making their eggs and chicks vulnerable to predation. Furthermore, the adult birds are unable to fly during the molting season, and thus are easily caught by foxes during this period. So severe was the impact of foxes on the Aleutian Canada goose population that not a single bird was observed during surveys of the Aleutians between 1938 and 1962. They were, indeed, thought to be extinct.

Jones was not convinced. In the words of Vernon Byrd, supervisory wildlife biologist at Alaska Maritime NWR, "Bob thought there might be geese left somewhere. He understood that the reason the geese had declined was the introduction of foxes on their nesting islands. As a result, Bob started trying to take foxes off one island so, if he ever found geese, he could either restore them or they would come back on their own. That was really sort of the beginning of the recovery program."

In 1962 Jones beached his dory on rugged Buldir Island, and there he found his Aleutian Canada geese. The island had escaped fox introductions because it has no protected coves or good landing beaches. Jones estimated that this goose population, which may have been all of the Aleutian Canada geese that remained in the world, numbered only 200 to 300 birds.

In March 1967 the Aleutian Canada goose was listed as endangered under the Endangered Species Protection Act of 1966, a precursor to today's Endangered Species Act.

Beginning in the 1970s, USFWS biologists began relocating birds from Buldir Island to other islands from which, following Jones's plan, foxes had been removed. This marked the beginning of a dramatic species recovery story.

In March 2001, with an estimated population of 37,000 birds nesting throughout most of its former range, the Aleutian Canada goose was declared recovered and removed from the list of endangered and threatened species.

Jones retired from USFWS in 1980, leaving a furred and feathered legacy in the refuge lands he managed that few have equaled. ■

This 1974 photo shows Bob "Sea Otter" Jones at Izembek Lagoon, where he studied waterfowl and the eelgrass beds on which they feed during migration. (Jim Rearden)

Alaska Peninsula NWR

Sandwiched between Becharof NWR to the north and Izembek NWR to the south, Alaska Peninsula NWR presents a dramatic landscape of active volcanoes, towering mountain peaks, rolling tundra, and rugged, wave-battered coasts. As is the case with most of Alaska's coastal refuges, salmon provide the principal "nutrient engine" for Alaska Peninsula, supporting species that prey on them and enriching rivers and surrounding lands after they spawn and die.

Upper and Lower Ugashik Lakes, connected by Ugashik Narrows, form the heart of the refuge's salmon production and are, respectively, the ninth and 11th largest of Alaska's lakes. They, along with the larger Becharof Lake system and other Alaska Peninsula refuge waters, are the nurseries for many of the Pacific salmon that support commercial fisheries on the Bering Sea and Pacific coasts from June through September each year.

Where there are salmon, there will usually be bears, and when the fish are running, Ugashik Lakes and the streams that surround them attract brown bears in great numbers. Brown and grizzly bears are the same species; coastal bears are generally referred to as brown, while inland are called grizzly. Black bears are not found on Alaska Peninsula NWR, but caribou, wolverine, wolf, and moose are. The latter are relative newcomers, first recorded on the peninsula in the early 1900s, and uncommon until the 1950s. The refuge's coastal and offshore waters are home to sea otters, harbor seals, sea lions, and migrating whales.

Alaska Peninsula's numerous wetlands and rocky shores provide habitat for migratory birds, including ducks, geese, and shorebirds. The refuge is also home to the westernmost black cottonwood forests in the United States, which offer migration stopover and nesting habitat for Neotropical land birds.

The region's rich wildlife populations have attracted human settlement for centuries. Archeological finds indicate that at least one village existed near the Ugashik Lakes as early as 9,000 years ago. Residents of this settlement apparently used all of the resources available to them, harvesting fish, birds, and mammals. Russians found Yup'ik and Alutiiq people on the central Alaska Peninsula, Dena'ina people in the Iliamna Lake region, and Unangan people on the lower Alaska Peninsula and in the Aleutian Islands living a subsistence lifestyle. At the time, trade goods from the region were reaching other parts of Alaska, the Pacific Northwest coast, and perhaps even other parts of North America and northeastern Asia. Russians added an intensified international fur trade, focused primarily on sea otter pelts, to the region's economy.

In latter years of the nineteenth century, as scarcity drove the fur industry into decline, salmon canneries became the area's new economic engine. However, residents continued to rely on subsistence. The history of the village of Ugashik effectively ended when the flu epidemic of 1919 reached the Alaska Peninsula.

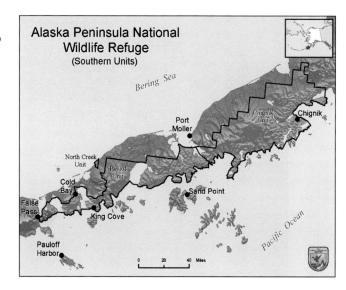

Alaska Peninsula National Wildlife Refuge (Southern Units)

Alaska Peninsula NWR

Established: 1980
Acreage: 3,500,605
Location: Alaska Peninsula

Bear trails converge on "rubbing boulders" along an Alaska Peninsula NWR salmon stream. In wooded areas, bears rub against trees, but on open tundra, rocks are sometimes the only objects large and solid enough to satisfy an itch. (John Sarvis)

Few residents survived, and those that did moved to other communities in the region.

Today, many of the area's rural people continue to depend on refuge resources — hunting, fishing, trapping, and gathering plants and berries as part of a subsistence lifestyle similar to that practiced by the earliest residents of the region. Many visitors to the Alaska Peninsula are also attracted by hunting and fishing. The brown bear is probably the refuge's most coveted hunting trophy, while anglers pursue salmon, arctic char, lake trout, northern pike, and grayling. Alaska's

Mount Veniaminof

Towering 8,225 feet above the waters of nearby Bristol Bay and with a base almost 22 miles across, Mount Veniaminof is a special link in a volcanic chain known as the Ring of Fire, which encircles the Pacific Ocean. It was designated an Historic Landmark in 1967. One of the world's largest and most active volcanoes, Veniaminof is a stratovolcano, characterized by a steep-sided cone shape containing alternating layers of lava, ash, and other volcanic materials. Many of Earth's largest and most explosive volcanoes share this structure.

Veniaminof's earliest known eruption, approximately 3,700 years ago, is believed to have been among the largest in history, and more than 50 times as violent as the May 18, 1980, Mount St. Helens eruption. At the peak of that event the mountain blew its top, forming a huge caldera approximately six miles across; an icefield covers the caldera today. Two young cinder cones poke through the ice, and one of these has been the site of the volcano's most recent eruptions, one in 1983-84 and another a decade later, both producing ash and lava flows that melted large pits in the icefield. In all, Veniaminof has erupted seven times during the last century, though none of these have come close to the violence of the caldera-forming eruption of 3,700 years ago. Still, some of these events were dramatic in their own right. During the June 1939 eruption, for example, ash reportedly fell to a thickness of an inch or more for more than 50 miles. Recent research indicates that at least one and perhaps two additional catastrophic eruptions might have occurred at Veniaminof prior to the eruption of 3,700 years ago.

In mid September 2002, Veniaminof again showed signs of seismic unrest. The Alaska Volcano Observatory actively monitors the volcano using satellite image analysis and data from a network of seismic stations that send a constant flow of information to scientists in Anchorage and Fairbanks. ■

Mount Veniaminof is one of the Alaska Peninsula's several active volcanoes. (Courtesy Alaska Volcano Observatory)

record grayling, a four pound, 13 ounce lunker, was caught in Ugashik Narrows by Paul F. Kanitz in 1981.

Other popular public uses of the refuge include flightseeing, wildlife observation and photography, hiking, backpacking, boating, and camping. There are no roads or established trails on the refuge, and access is typically by bush plane or boat. Aircraft charters and boat rentals are available in King Salmon, the site of refuge headquarters. ■

Sockeye salmon, bright red from time spent in fresh water, travel toward spawning grounds on the Alaska Peninsula. (Greg Syverson)

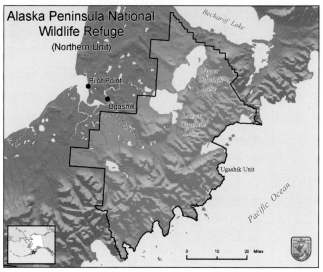

Alaska Peninsula National Wildlife Refuge (Northern Unit)

Arctic NWR

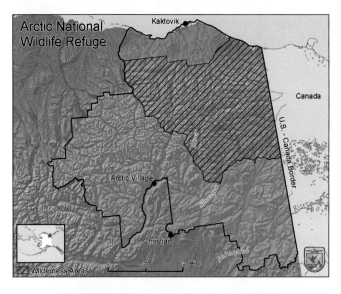

Arctic National Wildlife Refuge

Kaktovik

Canada

U.S. - Canada Border

Arctic Village

Sheenjek

River

Christian

Wilderness Areas

Arctic NWR

Established: 1960
Acreage: 19,285,922
Designated Wilderness: 8,000,000 acres
Wild and Scenic Rivers: Sheenjek, Ivishak, and Wind Rivers
Location: Northeast corner of Alaska from the Canning River east to Canada, and from the Beaufort Sea south to just below the Arctic Circle

In the 1950s, a new concept was taking hold among Americans concerned with protection of wild things and places. This notion marked the evolutionary divide between the conservation ethic that characterized that community before and the environmentalism to come. Put simply, the idea was that wilderness itself had a value over and above any utilitarian purposes it might serve, now or in the future.

The writings of such conservation leaders as Aldo Leopold and Robert Marshall helped shape this conviction, and a 1953 article in the journal *Sierra* entitled "Northeast Arctic, The Last Great Wilderness," focused the attention of this growing movement on arctic Alaska. The article's authors, National Park Service employees George Collins and Lowell Sumner, were convinced the northeastern corner of Alaska was one of the finest surviving examples of true wilderness, and with the help of Wilderness Society president Olaus Murie and his wife, Mardy, they campaigned for its protection.

The effort quickly gained support in the Lower 48 and Alaska. Even the *Fairbanks Daily News-Miner*, long a supporter of extractive industries, urged in an editorial that, in northeastern Alaska, "we will leave as heritage to the future something besides tin cans, dilapidated buildings, rust and an assortment of holes in the ground." On December 6, 1960, outgoing Pres. Dwight D. Eisenhower's secretary of the interior, Fred A. Seaton, established the nine-million-acre Arctic National Wildlife Range under Public Land Order 2214 for the "purpose of preserving unique wildlife, wilderness and recreational values."

Two decades later, ANILCA more than doubled the size of the wildlife range and renamed it Arctic National Wildlife Refuge, making it the largest refuge, containing the largest designated Wilderness area, in the national wildlife refuge system. Section 1002 of ANILCA also authorized a study of the oil and gas potential of the refuge's coastal plain as well as a "comprehensive and continuing inventory and assessment of the fish and wildlife resources of the coastal plain" and an analysis of the "potential effects of oil and gas exploration, development and production on such wildlife and habitats." Since then, the refuge's coastal plain has been known as the "ten-o-two" area. ANILCA further ordered, in Section 1003, that "production of oil and gas from the Arctic National Wildlife Refuge is prohibited and no leasing or other development leading to production of oil and gas from the range shall be undertaken until authorized by an Act of Congress." These two sections set the stage for an epic conservation battle that continues to this day.

The coastal plain has been conversely called a "frozen wasteland" and the "biological heart of the refuge." It is of vital importance to a wide variety of species, including resident muskox, the migratory Porcupine caribou herd, and the hundreds of thousands of birds that arrive in spring and summer to feed and nest before departing for wintering areas in Asia, South America, the South Pacific, and every U.S. state. The plain, however, is only one component of the refuge.

This most biologically diverse conservation unit in the circumpolar north was protected, in part, because it includes a complex succession of arctic habitat. From the boreal forest of the Porcupine River uplands to the foothills and barren peaks of the Brooks Range north to the arctic tundra of the coastal plain and the lagoons and barrier islands of the Beaufort Sea coast, the refuge's diversity supports 45 species of land and marine mammals, 36 species of fish, and 180 species of birds. It is the only U.S. conservation area in which all three North American bears — black, polar, and grizzly — can be found. It also contains traditional homelands and subsistence areas of Inupiaq Eskimos of the arctic coast and Athabascan Indians of the Interior.

Smoke rises from a cabin in the Brooks Range, which bisects Arctic NWR between the Dalton Highway and the Canadian border. (Stuart Pechek)

A northern harrier eats a freshly killed willow ptarmigan. Northern harriers hunt close to the ground for mice and small birds. (Steven Kazlowski)

Arctic NWR is the northernmost refuge in the nation. Snow cover is to be expected everywhere on the refuge from September to May. Even in midsummer, permafrost persists a few inches beneath the soil in many areas, causing meltwater and rain to saturate and pool atop the thin layer of thawed topsoil. Summer's constant daylight helps nourish a brief explosion of green, consisting of hundreds of species of mosses, grasses, wildflowers, shrubs, and other plants. The same conditions support an equally impressive "bloom" of insects during June and July.

The refuge is open to the public year-round. Most visitors take scheduled flights from Fairbanks to Fort Yukon, Kaktovik, or Deadhorse where charter flights are available into the refuge. There are also outfitters who guide expeditions for

Mardy and Olaus Murie

It would not be much of an overstatement to say that Arctic NWR owes its existence to the vision, hard work, and dedication of Olaus and Margaret (Mardy) Murie, or to say that the modern conservation movement was born of their 1924 marriage in Anvik, on the Yukon River. Considering the winding paths that led to their meeting, it's a wonder that Olaus and Mardy found each other at all.

He was born in Moorhead, Minnesota, in 1889, when that state was still part of the American frontier. The son of Norwegian immigrants, Olaus was inspired enough by the wild northwestern prairie to pursue a career in the natural sciences. He graduated from Oregon's Pacific University in 1912 with a background in zoology and wildlife biology, and immediately went to work as an Oregon state conservation officer. Subsequent

explorations in eastern Canada, supported by Pittsburgh's Carnegie Museum, helped educate and shape the young scientist/conservationist for what would become his life's work.

A native of Seattle, Margaret Thomas moved with her family to Fairbanks at an early age. She attended the University of Alaska there, becoming its first woman graduate in 1924. Growing up on the edge of the northern wilderness made a profound impression on the young woman and fueled a desire to protect the wild places that had been so important to her youth.

In 1920 Olaus took a position as a wildlife biologist with the U.S. Bureau of Biological Survey, a precursor of USFWS. It was in this capacity that he came to Alaska, charged with conducting a study of the territory's caribou herds. During this six-year project, he married the newly graduated Margaret Thomas. Their 500-mile honeymoon voyage began with a steamer journey up the Koyukuk River, after which the newlyweds set off into the Brooks Range by dogsled, continuing Olaus's research.

Describing the first adventure of their marriage in her book *Two in the Far North* (1962), Mardy wrote, "Days on the trail taught us that there is always and forever something to rejoice about. It was a fairyland, this highland, skyland, on a glorious blue-and-gold day. Our seven dogs, the

A canvas tent with woodstove served as home during Olaus and Mardy Murie's honeymoon in the Brooks Range in 1924. (Courtesy The Murie Center)

In 1956, the Muries guided fellow scientists and conservationists on the Sheenjek River, south of the Brooks Range, as part of their efforts to protect land in what is now Arctic NWR. From left to right are Olaus Murie, Justice William O. Douglas, Mardy Murie, and Mercedes Douglas. (Courtesy The Murie Center)

two of us, alone up there, sliding along the top of the world."

In 1927, after the conclusion of the caribou project, the bureau assigned Olaus to do a similarly comprehensive study of the Teton Mountain elk herd. The Muries established a permanent home, a base camp to adventure from, in Jackson Hole, Wyoming. As Olaus continued his work, both with the bureau and, after 1937, as a council member of the recently formed Wilderness Society, Mardy and the family accompanied him. During this period the couple's advocacy for the protection of wild places bore fruit, and their influence contributed to the expansion of Washington state's Olympic National Monument and the creation of Jackson Hole National Monument in Wyoming.

Olaus left the Biological Survey in 1945 to serve as director of the Wilderness Society. It was during this period that he and Mardy, encouraged by Lowell Sumner and George Collins, began to work specifically for protection of lands that are now part of the Arctic NWR. These efforts culminated in their 1956 Sheenjek expedition, when the Muries guided a group of scientists and prominent voices in the conservation community into the Brooks Range. The trip laid the groundwork for creation of a conservation area that includes an entire spectrum of arctic ecosystems. It was, Mardy recalls, "a perfect expedition." It was the last such journey this remarkable couple made together.

Olaus lived to see the creation of Arctic National Wildlife Range in 1960; it was, Mardy says, only the second time she had ever seen him cry. He died in 1963, just months before passage of the Wilderness Act that owed so much to his ideas and tireless advocacy.

Mardy has continued the work she and Olaus shared. She joined the governing council of the Wilderness Society and in that capacity testified before Congress in favor of ANILCA, saying, in part, "I am testifying as an emotional woman and I would like to ask you, gentlemen, what's wrong with emotion? Beauty is a resource in and of itself. Alaska must be allowed to be Alaska, that is her greatest economy. I hope that America is not so rich that she can afford to let these wildernesses pass by, or so poor that she cannot afford to keep them."

Mardy celebrated her 100th birthday on August 18, 2002. ∎

recreation, hunting, or fishing to the refuge. Would-be visitors can obtain a list of approved services by contacting refuge headquarters in Fairbanks.

The refuge is, however, extremely remote and demands the fullest attention of even the most experienced backcountry adventurer. Emergency supplies and extra food are essential, as an air taxi that drops off passengers might be delayed by weather for several days past the arranged pickup date. Visitors should leave no trace of passing so those that come after can enjoy the same experience of traveling through untouched wilderness that inspired the refuge's founders. Conscientious travel also assures that this wild place maintains its value as a laboratory where scientists can study the natural dynamics of an unaltered land. ∎

Polar bears inhabit coastal regions of Arctic NWR and are the largest nonaquatic carnivores in the world. (Steven Kazlowski)

Porcupine Caribou Herd

The migration of the Porcupine caribou herd is one of the world's great wildlife spectacles, comparable to the massed wanderings of Africa's wildebeest. Twice each year, in spring and fall, the herd of more than 120,000 animals sets off on a journey of nearly 800 miles, covering as much as 50 miles a day. That 800-mile figure, though impressive, reflects only the straight-line mileage between the two most distant migration points.

Satellite monitoring of Porcupine herd cows indicates that, in their meandering travels, they can range up to 3,100 miles a year, among the longest migrations of the world's land mammals.

Though often referred to as "porcupine caribou," members of the Porcupine herd are barrenground caribou, and take their name not from any resemblance to the prickly rodent but from the Porcupine River, which the herd often crosses during migration. It is the third largest of Alaska's 32 caribou herds, or populations, which are defined as groups of animals that share a distinct and separate calving area, though members of more than one herd might intermingle on their wintering grounds.

The Porcupine herd's range, which includes portions of Canada's Yukon and Northwest Territories as well as much of Arctic NWR, covers an area the size of Wyoming. The Latin name for caribou, *Rangifer*, means "wanderer," and the calendar of the Porcupine herd is a story of constant travel.

The animals winter in the southern portion of their territory, south of the Brooks Range in Alaska and Canada, where they provide a valuable source of subsistence food for the Gwitch'in Athabascans. The long, dark months are a difficult time for the herd, and fat accumulated during the rest of the year can be key to winter survival. Food can be scarce. What is available is relatively poor in nutrition and not easily digestible and often can only be reached by scraping away a deep cover of snow. This behavior, perhaps, prompted the name "caribou," which is presumed to be a corruption of the northeastern Micmac word "xalibu," or "the one who paws."

Migrating caribou from the Porcupine herd cross the Kongakut River. Hollow guard hairs increase buoyancy and enable the animals to swim for some distance with ease. This group is shedding its thick winter coat. (Tom Bol Photography)

In early March the herd begins to move again. At first the spring migration seems to be little more than a general wandering toward the northernmost reaches of the wintering range. As the days grow longer in April, though, the migration begins to take on an urgency. Cows that are carrying calves, accompanied by barren females and some yearlings, are the first to strike out, taking one of three major routes north. The bulls and remaining young animals follow a week or more later. It is fitting that pregnant cows provide the impetus for this journey, because almost two months and as much as 400 miles later, it will end on the herd's calving ground.

Although the area in which Porcupine herd cows have historically given birth includes the northern foothills of the Brooks Range and the arctic coastal plain from Alaska's Tamayariak River to the Babbage River in Canada, the most commonly used calving area is on the coastal plain of Arctic NWR, between the Katakturuk and Kongakut Rivers. Studies conducted from 1982 through 2001 showed that calving was concentrated on the coastal plain during 11 of those 19 years. When lingering or late snows prevent the herd from reaching its preferred calving ground, the calves suffer. 2001 was such a year, and the Alaska Department of Fish and Game (ADFG) reported that at the end of June, only between 44 percent and 51 percent of cows were accompanied by calves, the lowest rate of calf survival recorded during more than 20 years of research on the herd.

The coastal plain offers several advantages that foster herd health and calf survival. First of all, the plain is rich in cottongrass, and immature cottongrass flowers are extremely high in nutrients and more easily digestible than moss and evergreen shrub forage available elsewhere in the herd's calving range. Green-up on the coastal plain typically coincides with calving, when a source of nutritious, digestible food is especially important to pregnant cows. It is certainly welcomed by other members of the herd as well, after the long semifast of the winter. Additionally, predators, primarily brown bears, wolves, and golden eagles, are less numerous on the flat, exposed coastal plain than in the adjacent foothills and mountains, reducing the impact of predation on calves. Because barrenground caribou have a brief breeding period, about two weeks, their calves are born over a short period as well, usually between the last week in May and the second week in June. This fact also limits the number of calves killed by predators. A more drawn-out birth period would produce consecutive groups of very young animals, leaving immature calves vulnerable to predators over a longer period of time.

After the calves are born the caribou form what are known as postcalving aggregations. During this time the entire herd typically gathers on the coastal plain. Even during years when late snowmelt prevents the caribou from reaching the plain for calving, they continue to move toward the refuge's coast during this postcalving period. Until late June to mid July, the caribou feed on the coastal plain. There is evidence that this postcalving feeding is far more important to the Porcupine herd than to some other populations. For example, the adjacent Central Arctic caribou herd obtains only about one-fourth as much of its annual dietary nitrogen from its calving ground as does the Porcupine herd.

In addition to providing nutritious forage, the flat coastal plain is typically breezier and cooler

A caribou's eyes have little sensitivity to color or form, but they detect movement well. The species seems to rely mostly on its sense of smell. (Robin Brandt)

than the surrounding uplands at this time of year, providing relief from mosquitoes that emerge in late June or early July. Caribou avoiding these insects sometimes gather in great numbers. In 1987, a group estimated to contain more than 93,000 animals was seen clustered south of Camden Bay.

By mid July most of the herd will have moved into the foothills and mountains to the south of the coastal plain, where they feed until beginning the fall migration, which can start as early as the end of August or as late as October. This return journey, which is not interrupted even for the brief October rut, will carry them again south of the Brooks Range, where they will wait through winter, until spring and the call of the calving ground summons them north again. ∎

Becharof NWR

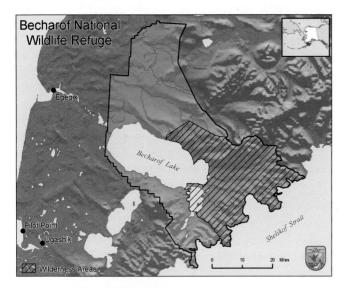

Becharof National Wildlife Refuge

Egegik

Becharof Lake

Pilot Point
Ugashik

Shelikof Strait

0   10   20 Miles

Wilderness Areas

Becharof NWR

Established: 1980
Acreage: 1,200,017
Designated Wilderness: 400,000 acres
Location: Base of the Alaska Peninsula, between Katmai National Park and Preserve and Alaska Peninsula NWR

Becharof NWR is a land of contrasts. From its rugged coasts to the 4,835-foot summit of volcanic Mount Peulik, the refuge includes everything from tundra to braided, glacier-fed rivers to saw-toothed mountain ranges. But few would argue that the biological heart of the refuge is the lake that bears its name.

Becharof Lake is huge — 35 miles long, 15 miles wide, and as much as 600 feet deep — and is fed by two major rivers and numerous creeks. This second biggest lake in Alaska and the largest in the entire national wildlife refuge system is a veritable salmon factory. The 300,000-acre lake serves as a nursery for the world's second largest run of sockeye salmon. It's estimated that Becharof Lake and its tributaries provide the Bristol Bay fishery alone with as many as six million adult salmon per year. When the waters of adjacent Alaska Peninsula NWR are added to the equation, the numbers become more dramatic still: The two refuges produce more than 30 million fish annually.

Studies underway at Becharof Lake are contributing to an understanding of the cyclical nature of salmon runs. Scientists read layers of sediment deposited on the bottom of the lake over the past 300 years and estimate, from those layers created by the annual decomposition of salmon, the size of that year's run. University of Alaska researchers have found evidence that suggests climate change and climatic patterns may play more important roles than previously thought in influencing the ups and downs of sockeye production.

When Becharof's salmon are spawning, they attract one of the largest concentrations of brown bears in Alaska. Becharof and Alaska Peninsula Refuges combined are thought to be home to as many as 3,000 of these animals. When not lured to the refuge's lakes and streams by spawning salmon, bears roam all of the refuge, feeding on plants, berries, ground squirrels, moose, caribou, and carrion, depending on the season.

Moose are present on the refuge in moderate, and seemingly increasing, numbers. Caribou of the Northern Alaska Peninsula herd migrate through, and winter on, Becharof. This herd has fluctuated dramatically, varying from a low of 2,000 to a high of 20,000 during the last half of the twentieth century. It currently stands at less than 10,000. Wolverine, fox, river otter, and beaver round out the list of larger land animals, while harbor seals, sea lions, sea otters, and whales are found offshore. Seabirds, as well as eagles and peregrine falcons, nest on the refuge's coastal cliffs, and migratory waterfowl use the wetlands and estuaries as nesting grounds and staging areas on the way

FACING PAGE: *Ancient layers of rock outcrop on the Alaska Peninsula at Dry Bay, near the southern corner of Becharof NWR. Obvious geological formations abound in this seismically active region.*
(John Bauman)

Ukinrek Maars

Between March 30 and April 10, 1977, a low ridge about a mile south of Becharof Lake was the site of a geological event unique in the history of the United States. During that time, two *maars*, low, broad, volcanic craters, formed.

Ukinrek Maars are thought to have been caused when rising magma encountered groundwater trapped in layers of pumice-rich deposits from nearby Ugashik Caldera and glacial till, a mixture of

An aerial view looking southeast shows Ukinrek Maars, two holes formed in 1977 when magma boiled groundwater, causing explosions at the surface. Mount Peulik, beyond, was last volcanically active in 1852. (R.J. Wilk, courtesy USFWS)

gravel, clay, and other materials produced by the grinding action of moving ice. The resulting steam explosions, called phreatomagmatic events, effectively blew two huge holes in the landscape. West Maar, the first to form, is approximately 550 feet in diameter and up to 100 feet deep; East Maar is about 900 feet in diameter and as much as 200 feet deep. It features an almost 160-foot-high scoria cone, or lava dome, in its center, which has been covered by the crater lake that formed as groundwater seeped into this *maar*.

During the days of volcanic activity that formed Ukinrek Maars, steam and plumes of ash shot almost 20,000 feet into the air, and blocks of rock were tossed as far as 2,000 feet. Since the eruption, CO_2 gas has continued to be emitted from the area around the *maars*, as well as from beneath Becharof Lake, in a constant reminder that the lands of Becharof NWR are still being shaped. ∎

to and from nest sites in the Arctic.

Many visitors come to Becharof NWR for the outstanding hunting, primarily for brown bears. Sportfishing is also popular. In addition to all North American species of Pacific salmon, the refuge's lakes, rivers, and streams contain arctic grayling, Dolly Varden, rainbow and lake trout, burbot, and northern pike. Other popular recreational activities include hiking and camping, which can provide abundant opportunities for wildlife observation and photography. Outfitters, air charter, and flightseeing services can be found in King Salmon. ∎

Numerous brown bears live in Becharof NWR; they feed on spawning salmon, small and large land mammals, greens, berries, and carrion. The Alaska Peninsula supports about 45 bears per 100 square miles. (John Bauman)

Bordered by the Yukon River on the west, the Kuskokwim Mountains on the east and south and the Khotol Hills on the north, with the Innoko River at its center, Innoko NWR can be roughly divided into two habitat types. Approximately half of the refuge consists of black spruce muskeg, wet meadows, and sedge or horsetail marshes, set with innumerable lakes and ponds of varying size. The rest of the terrain is marked by hills, most of which are less than 1,000 feet. Because these slopes are well-drained and thus for the most part free from permafrost, they support stands of white spruce, paper birch, and aspen. Northern Innoko NWR, commonly known as Kaiyuh Flats, is managed as part of the Koyukuk/Nowitna refuge complex. Rich in wetlands, the Northern Innoko is an extremely productive breeding area for migratory waterfowl and fish. The Innoko Wilderness is bordered by the Innoko River on its western boundary and includes portions of the Iditarod and Big and Little Yetna Rivers. Several abandoned gold-rush-era towns exist within the refuge's boundaries, but no people permanently inhabit its lands today. There are only gold-rush-era roads on Innoko, and no designated trails.

The poorly drained lowlands and colder, north-facing slopes typically sport stunted black spruce woodland with an understory

Beavers inhabit most forested regions of Alaska, including Innoko NWR. During the late 1800s, almost three million beavers were trapped in Alaska, the pelts sold to England. Trappers still harvest these furs here today. (George Matz)

of lichens, mosses, and shrubs. Willow and alder crowd the edges of most rivers and streams and border the refuge's abundant low meadows and marshes. To the west, banks and islands of the Yukon support a collage of white spruce, paper birch, cottonwood, and aspen.

Given the extensive wetlands contained within the refuge, it comes as no surprise that Innoko is blessed with a wealth of avian life. Scientists estimate that 130 bird species use these lands, and that more than 300,000 waterfowl and shorebirds nest on them every spring. White-fronted geese, lesser Canada geese, pintails, northern shovelers, greater and lesser scaups, mallards, green-winged

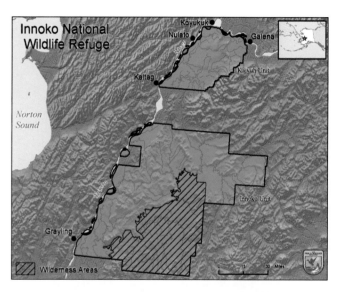

Innoko NWR

Established: 1980
Acreage: 3,850,321; Northern Innoko: 751,000
Designated Wilderness: 1,240,000 acres
Location: Central Yukon River Valley; Northern Innoko NWR: Yukon River floodplain, south of the Yukon River and North of the Kaiyuh Mountains in westcentral Alaska

LEFT: *Volunteer Lynn Neibaur bands a pintail duck in Innoko NWR. Ongoing studies in Alaska's national wildlife refuges help determine health, population, and activity of various species. (Tom Walker)*

ABOVE: *Tracks in the snow reveal the Innoko region's abundant animal life. (Courtesy USFWS)*

teals, greater and lesser yellowlegs, Hudsonian godwits, and black, surf, and white-winged scoters need the wetlands. In fact, so important a nursery is the Innoko NWR that its summer waterfowl counts are used to help set fall hunting regulations from Alaska to Mexico.

Frequent flooding of rivers and streams on the refuge helps fertilize surrounding soils and maintains the rich willow sandbar habitat that provides winter food for an abundant moose population, as well as for beaver, which are common along all of Innoko's rivers and streams. Approximately 40 percent of the beaver trapped in

Alaska come from the refuge. Barren-ground caribou from the Beaver Mountain herd winter on Innoko when deep snows move them down from the uplands, while black and grizzly bears and wolves are present year-round. Other furbearers include marten, lynx, red fox, river otter, and wolverine.

Although Innoko is open to public use, its isolation and lack of facilities limit the number of visitors. Trappers from nearby Yukon River villages use the refuge in winter, and some bird hunting is done by subsistence users. Since the Iditarod Trail, a winter-only trail, passes through Innoko, parts of the refuge see a flurry of activity when the famous sled dog race comes through.

Floating the Innoko River offers excellent opportunities to view and photograph the abundant wildlife, and is a common means of accessing the refuge by hunters and anglers. Innoko's healthy moose populations attract hunters from throughout Alaska and around the world.

It's also possible to access the refuge by chartered aircraft out of Anchorage, McGrath, Bethel, or Galena. Since much of the refuge, particularly areas accessible by raft or floatplane, is low-lying marsh and bog, hip boots are recommended. The temperature in the summer can range from the 80s (Fahrenheit) to below freezing, and rain is common. The presence of hoards of mosquitoes and other biting bugs demands that anyone visiting in insect season carry good repellant, a headnet, and a mosquito-tight tent. In general, all of the commonsense rules for traveling in wilderness, and notably in bear country, apply here. ∎

Gold Fever!

The lure of gold helped shape Alaska, and images from the state's numerous strikes are among the most enduring in its history. The works of Jack London and Robert Service, as well as the humor of W.C. Fields, have immortalized this period. The Chilkoot Trail's infamous Golden Stairs, steps carved into snow at the top of Chilkoot Pass, are even pictured on some state license plates.

In the first years of the twentieth century, gold fever came to Innoko country, and soon after the first traces of color gleamed in the bottom of swirled pans, towns sprouted around each new discovery. Ophir and McGrath grew on the back of the September 1906 gold strikes on Ganes Creek and, later, on Ophir Creek. Three more towns — Flat, Dikeman, and Iditarod — rose in the wake of the 1908 discovery of gold in Otter Creek, a tributary of the Iditarod River.

Many of these boomtowns were temporary, waxing and waning with the strike that supported them, and their remnants can be found on the refuge today. By floating portions of the Innoko River, travelers can visit the remains of such gold-rush towns as Simels Roadhouse, Rennies Landing, Cripple Landing, and Dishkaket. At Simels Roadhouse, foundation logs are still visible, as is the skeleton of an abandoned steamboat settling among riverside willows. Old buildings and a distinctive Russian Orthodox cemetery still stand in Dishkaket, originally an Athabascan winter village that grew with the gold boom and was abandoned in the mid 1920s.

"Color" can still be found along sandbars of the Innoko itself and at the mouths of creeks and rivers flowing into the main course. Visitors will better understand the power of the fever that built these towns when they see those bright flakes winking among the sand in their own pans.

On the other hand, a savvy prospector will pack along some fishing gear as well as a gold pan. After all, there's more than one sort of treasure to be found in the Innoko River. One could certainly say that angler Jack Wagner "struck it rich" in 1991 when he landed a 38-pound northern pike, a monster that still holds the Alaska record. ∎

Gold was found in the Innoko region in 1906 and again in 1908, causing thousands to rush to the fledgling town of Iditarod in search of riches. That stampede helped form the Iditarod Trail, which passes through Innoko NWR. (Tom Bundtzen)

Izembek NWR

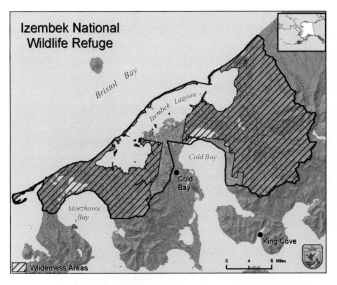

Izembek National Wildlife Refuge

Bristol Bay

Izembek Lagoon

Cold Bay

Cold Bay

Morzhovoi Bay

King Cove

Wilderness Areas

0   4   8 Miles

Izembek NWR

Established: 1960
Acreage: 311,075
Designated Wilderness: 307,981 acres
Location: Tip of the Alaska Peninsula

Izembek is the smallest of Alaska's refuges. At its heart is 150-square-mile Izembek Lagoon, named after the surgeon of the Russian sloop *Moller*, which sailed around the world in the late 1820s. Here,

A spotted seal pup rests at Cape Krenitzin, on the Bering Sea coast in Izembek NWR. Spotted seals weigh 15 to 20 pounds at birth and reach adult weights of 150 to 250 pounds. (John Sarvis)

shallow, brackish water covers one of the world's largest beds of eelgrass, a haven for migrating birds. So important are the lagoon and its underwater pastures that in 1986 it was one of the first sites in the United States to be designated a Wetland of International Importance by the

RAMSAR Convention on Wetlands, first held in Ramsar, Iran. In March 2001, the American Bird Conservancy designated Izembek refuge a Globally Important Bird Area. The state-owned tidal lands and the submerged lands beneath the lagoon are protected by the State of Alaska as the Izembek State Game Refuge. In addition to hosting 98 percent of the world's Pacific brant twice a year, Izembek Lagoon is an important migration stopover for the world's population of more than 62,000 emperor geese and an important molting area for approximately 23,000 Steller's eiders, a species that is currently listed as threatened under the Endangered Species Act.

Among the 186 species of birds that have been observed on or adjacent to the refuge are lesser golden plovers and ruddy turnstones from the South Pacific, semipalmated plovers and western sandpipers from South America, tundra swans and rock sandpipers that remain on the refuge year-round, and McKay's bunting, a species endemic to western Alaska.

Although the lagoon can certainly be called the centerpiece of Izembek NWR, it is only one piece of the mosaic of habitats contained within its boundaries. From the waters of the Bering Sea to the 6,600-foot summit of glacier-capped, volcanic Frosty Peak, the refuge's lands consist primarily of wetlands covered in low brush and tundra, but include lagoons, lakes, ponds, and streams; lowlands thick with alder; and barren, glacier-shouldered mountains.

King, pink, red, chum, and silver salmon fill the streams in a series of runs lasting from summer into early fall. These, in turn, lure brown bears to the banks where they can feast on fish. At times during the salmon runs brown bear densities along certain streams can be as high as six animals per square mile, among the highest recorded anywhere.

The Southern Alaska Peninsula caribou herd, with approximately 3,000 animals, also roams the refuge. Moose, wolves, foxes, and other furbearers occur here as well. In addition, several species of marine mammals either inhabit or pass through refuge coastal waters and lagoons. These include threatened Steller sea lions, harbor seals, sea otters, walrus, and gray and minke whales.

There are no inhabited villages within

BELOW: *Hunter and photographer James L. Davis rests with his yellow lab, Tule, in Izembek NWR. (James L. Davis)*

RIGHT: *Pacific brant fatten on eelgrass at Izembek Lagoon before continuing to wintering grounds. Here, Amak Island, northwest of the lagoon, rises in the distance behind a flock. (John Sarvis)*

Izembek NWR today, but stubborn depressions in the tundra mark the sites of dwellings used by wandering Aleut peoples in the past. They navigated the coasts of the Alaska Peninsula in pursuit of marine resources for food, clothing, and shelter. Europeans first reached the shores of what is today Izembek refuge in the eighteenth century and established fur trading posts in the area. Today, descendants of these people share the

villages of Nelson Lagoon, King Cove, and False Pass with descendants of Aleuts who first traveled the region's waters. These three communities grew around salmon canneries established in the early twentieth century. A military base, Fort Randall, was built at the present site of Cold Bay during World War II and once housed as many as 20,000 troops.

Today, visitors come to Izembek NWR to hunt, fish, view and photograph the

incredible concentrations of wildlife, or simply to enjoy wilderness adventure. Backcountry travelers need to be "bear aware," especially when salmon are running, and be prepared for inclement weather: Izembek NWR experiences an average annual wind speed of 18 miles an hour and three feet of precipitation a year.

As is always the case when venturing far into wild refuge lands, it is best to consult with refuge staff while planning an Izembek adventure. ∎

Pacific Brant

It is rare for one relatively small piece of habitat to be essential to the health of a species, but that sort of relationship exists between the Izembek Lagoon complex and the Pacific brant. Twice each year, the world's population of these small sea geese pauses at the Izembek Lagoon complex to rest and fatten before continuing migration. This period of recuperation and refueling is particularly critical during fall migration. Then, typically riding the southerly winds of a low pressure system, most of the birds leave Izembek within a 12-hour period, setting off on nonstop journeys of up to 3,000 miles to their wintering areas. Brant can maintain average speeds of more than 50 miles per hour on these transoceanic supermarathons and lose about a third of their body weight during the trip.

The Pacific brant is a bird of the coast. It typically breeds in colonies near the tidal zone in the Yukon-Kuskokwim Delta, as well as along the high arctic coasts of Alaska, Canada, and Russia. Brant that breed in Russia winter on the coast of Asia. The fall migration, usually fully underway by early September, typically follows the coast south before pausing for up to nine weeks at Izembek Lagoon in preparation for the final leg of the trip to the brants' wintering grounds, most of which are in northwestern Mexico. Historically, a few brant have overwintered at Izembek. However, during the last two decades the numbers have increased and now more than 10 percent of the population overwinters here, making Izembek

A pair of Pacific brant tends their newly hatched chicks. The world's population of brant passes through Izembek NWR during migration. (Courtesy USFWS)

even more important to this species. As early as February, brant of breeding age, two to three years, that did migrate south begin to fly north, pausing at staging areas along the coast of western North America before again gathering at Izembek Lagoon by mid April. The flocks pause at the lagoon for as long as a month before returning to nesting areas to the north.

The Pacific brant population has been declining slowly for the past 40 years, with some biologists speculating their numbers decreased by more than 20 percent since the 1960s. During the same period, the birds largely abandoned traditional coastal wintering grounds from Puget Sound to California, preferring to winter in

lagoons along the Mexican coast of the Baja Peninsula and the Gulf of California. Degradation of habitats in the Pacific states, including loss of submerged aquatic vegetation and increased human disturbance, may have contributed to this shift. Though the abandonment of the western coastal wintering grounds does seem to coincide with the species decline, no direct connection has been proved.

It is clear, however, that the birds are sensitive to disturbance, which reduces foraging time and increases activity, potentially dangerous to a species with such a demanding migration. Aircraft are the most frequent causes of disturbance while the brant are staging in Izembek NWR. A predictive model developed by USFWS indicated that if brant were to be disturbed 11 times or more daily they would be unable to gain enough weight to survive migration to their wintering areas. Aircraft disturbance is currently below this level, but other factors, including boat traffic and eagles, also disturb the birds. Overall levels of disturbance are increasing on the Izembek complex and could someday harm the brant.

While biologists continue to study Pacific brant with the aim of understanding, and eventually stemming and reversing, their population decline, people can be grateful that the one piece of habitat most essential to that process, the eelgrass pastures beneath Izembek Lagoon, are surrounded by a piece of the national wildlife refuge system. ∎

Kanuti NWR

Kanuti NWR is, at 1,430,159 acres, approximately the size of Delaware. It sits atop the Arctic Circle, with about a third of the refuge above that meridian and two-thirds below. No roads or development exist in this wild land tucked into a basin drained by the Kanuti and Koyukuk Rivers and bordered to the north by foothills of the Brooks Range and to the south by the Ray Mountains. This bowl of gently rolling terrain, commonly referred to as Kanuti Flats, consists primarily of boreal forest, or taiga, studded with innumerable lakes, ponds, and marshes.

Kanuti's taiga, characterized by small and hardy examples of black and white spruce, aspen, birch, and cottonwood, is part of the planet's largest terrestrial eco-system, which arcs around the Northern Hemisphere across Canada, Scandinavia, and Asia. The taiga that characterizes Kanuti is relatively young in geologic time. Studies conducted by USGS of the Alaska fossil plant record indicate environmental responses to past periods of global climate change have been especially dramatic at these high latitudes. The record suggests that, through successions of warming and cooling, the areas now covered by boreal forest went through cycles during which the land was at times blanketed by tundra. Such temperate hardwoods as oak and hickory also grew here prior to about 10,000 years ago at the onset of the Holocene, the warm, interglacial period of today.

Warm, interglacial period or not, Kanuti NWR is still a place of extremes. Its annual temperature fluctuation, for example, ranges from minus 70 degrees Fahrenheit to higher than 90 degrees.

Alaska's wolves range from black to nearly white, with every shade of gray and tan between. Most adult males weigh from 85 to 115 pounds. Females average five to 10 pounds less. Kanuti NWR's wolves share the region with many other mammal species. (John Schwieder)

Short, hot summers give rise to numerous thunderstorms, and lightning strikes the dry taiga frequently. As a result, Kanuti's boreal forest burns on a 70-to-200-year cycle, making some of the refuge's lands

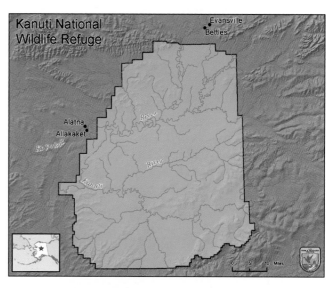

Kanuti National Wildlife Refuge

Kanuti NWR
Established: 1980
Acreage: 1,430,159
Location: 150 miles northwest of Fairbanks

the most fire-prone in Alaska. More than a third of Kanuti has burned since 1990. This continuous cycle of burn and recovery creates diverse habitats as different plant species, and levels of maturity within each

species, characterize the older and younger burns. The resulting habitat mosaic supports a variety of wildlife.

The refuge's migratory fish — sheefish and chinook, chum, and coho salmon — are creatures of extremes themselves. Kanuti's salmon travel more than 1,000 miles up the Yukon before entering the Koyukuk River system, which runs through the heart of the refuge, to spawn. Refuge waters support 12 other fish species, including grayling and northern pike.

Protecting breeding habitat for migratory birds is central to Kanuti's mission. Nearly 160 species of birds spend part or all of the year on refuge lands, including 50 species of waterfowl and shorebirds that migrate along four North American flyways and winter as far south as Mexico. With the loss of wetlands due to drought and the actions of man in regions to the south, the importance of Kanuti as a nesting area for waterfowl is likely to increase.

The refuge is also home to 37 species of mammals, including grizzly and black bear, several wolf packs, moose, wolverine, beaver, muskrat, marten, and mink. Caribou from the Western Arctic and Ray Mountain herds occasionally winter on Kanuti.

The refuge's combination of wildlife and scenery offers rich opportunities for outdoor recreation, including fishing, hunting, camping, boating, and photography. However, though the Dalton Highway passes just 10 miles to the east of the refuge, access is difficult. Few people visit Kanuti other than residents of the nearby villages of Alatna, Allakaket, Bettles, Evansville, and the surrounding area who use the refuge's subsistence resources. Because of this, the adventurous recreational traveler who does venture into this refuge will find unspoiled wildlands to rival those anywhere in Alaska.

Regular flights from Fairbanks service Allakaket and Bettles, and air taxis can be hired to fly travelers to the refuge from Bettles. Those who do visit Kanuti should be prepared for a completely unsupported wilderness adventure. Would-be river floaters, as well as any other visitors, are encouraged to speak to refuge staff while planning their trips to learn more about conditions on the ground, including the status of the rivers to be traveled, since many of these can't be navigated at certain flows. ■

Greater White-fronted Goose

The population of greater white-fronted geese that nests on Kanuti NWR appears to be declining. These interior-northwestern Alaska white-fronts, which also nest on Koyukuk, Nowitna, Innoko, Selawik, Yukon Flats, and Tetlin NWRs, as well as on adjacent lands, are a unique segment of the species' population. Their uniqueness stems from their nesting habitat, which is mainly in openings in the boreal forest and forest edge. The birds also migrate earlier, both in spring and fall, and use a more southerly and westerly wintering area, largely in the highlands of northern Mexico, than do other populations.

This medium-sized goose takes its name from the white patch that runs around the sides of the bill and on its forehead. The birds also have a distinctive pink bill and orange legs.

In recent years, traditional knowledge and modern research have indicated that the interior-northwestern Alaska population of white-fronts may be in decline. During oral interviews, Athabascan and Inupiaq elders have been consistent in their view that fewer geese were returning in the spring than had in seasons past. This observation was reinforced by USFWS's 2000 and 2001 aerial surveys of this breeding population, which suggested that white-fronted goose numbers had dropped by as much as 30 percent in the last two decades.

Reasons for this decline are not yet known. Current theories are based on the timing and route of the interior white-fronts' migration. It may be that, because the birds are among the first to migrate in the fall, their early arrival makes them more vulnerable to sport hunting in Alaska, Canada, Texas, and Mexico. Similarly, since they're among the first birds to arrive in the Interior in spring, they may bear a disproportionate brunt of the subsistence harvest. Estimates have placed the total sport-hunt harvest at more than 20 percent of the population, while subsistence hunters may have taken more than five percent of the population in recent years. Avian cholera is another suspect. The geese share wintering grounds with snow geese and other waterfowl, and since they tend to winter in relatively arid habitats, concentrations of birds on limited wetlands might increase the incidence of this disease. In the spring, the interior-northwestern Alaska population typically stops in Nebraska's Rainwater Basin, where avian cholera has been a recurring problem. As many as 10,000 white-fronts have died in a single year during outbreaks at this stopover.

So far, scientists can only speculate. But studies are underway at Kanuti and Koyukuk refuges, as well as along the birds' migration route, to determine what is happening to interior Alaska's white-fronted geese. With that information, wildlife managers can take steps to ensure that the high-pitched, laughing call of white-fronts continues to signal the long-awaited interior spring for generations. ■

LEFT: *Greater white-fronted geese average about six pounds. Their upper plumage ranges from gray-brown at the front to a dark brown tail, edged with white. Another white streak runs just below each wing. The breast feathers are lighter gray with brown and black markings, which inspired one of the white-front's common names, "specklebelly." (Tom Walker)*

RIGHT: *The three-note call of the greater white-fronted goose lends the species the nickname "laughing geese." They are also known as "orange-footed geese" by the Kanuti region's subsistence hunters. (Tom Walker)*

Kenai NWR

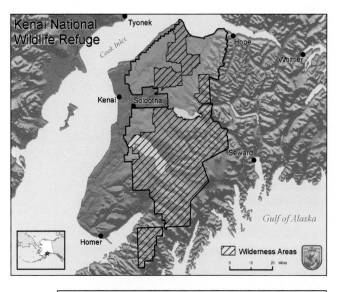

Kenai National Wildlife Refuge

Tyonek
Hope
Cook Inlet
Whittier
Kenai
Soldotna
Seward
Gulf of Alaska
Homer

Wilderness Areas
0   10   20 Miles

Kenai NWR

Established: 1941
Acreage: 1,908,127
Designated Wilderness: 1,350,000 acres
Location: 110 miles south of Anchorage,
    on the Sterling Highway

Alaska's Kenai Peninsula is still quite young in geologic terms, since its entire land mass was covered by glacial ice as recently as 10,000 years ago. Much of that frozen blanket still exists, in the form of the more than 800-square-mile Harding Icefield, which the refuge shares with Kenai Fjords National Park. This huge remnant of the Pleistocene ice age, when a glacial sheet covered much of North America, is the source of approximately 30 existing glaciers. At its deepest point, high in the eastern Kenai Mountains, the icefield is still thousands of feet thick.

The withdrawal of the Harding Icefield has helped make the lands of Kenai NWR a miniature Alaska. Today, the refuge includes examples of every major Alaska habitat type. Descending from the edges of the ice, a traveler would traverse treeless alpine and subalpine habitat, pass through boreal forest, and at lower elevations, encounter rivers, lakes, and wetlands, leading to the Kenai Peninsula's only remaining pristine saltwater estuary, the Chickaloon River Flats.

The refuge is also an Alaska in miniature in its diversity of wildlife. In addition to the sport fish that bring hundreds of thousands of visitors to the peninsula each year in pursuit of chinook, sockeye, coho, and pink salmon, northern pike, Dolly Varden, rainbow trout, grayling, and steelhead, the refuge is home to grizzly and black bears, caribou, Dall sheep, mountain goats, wolves, lynx, wolverines, eagles, and thousands of shorebirds and waterfowl, not to mention moose.

Today, Kenai NWR's wealth of habitat, scenery, and wildlife draws half a million visitors per year, more than any other refuge in the state. Kenai is one of only two Alaska refuges accessible by road; the other is Tetlin. A two-and-one-half-hour drive along the Seward and Sterling Highways south from Anchorage is the most common means of reaching the refuge.

Although the lure of huge runs of salmon may be the most obvious reason people visit Kenai NWR, its recreational opportunities are as varied as its habitats and wildlife. There are more than 50 miles of trails and hiking routes on the refuge, and these range from the easy Egumen Lake Trail and strenuous Fuller Lakes Trail to extended wilderness adventures. Anglers not wanting to compete for the prized salmon can explore the backcountry for arctic char, grayling, Dolly Varden, and rainbow trout. In addition to the hiking trails, the refuge's Dave Spencer Wilderness Unit includes the Swan Lake and Swanson River canoe trail systems, each of which offer more than 100 miles of linked rivers, streams, lakes, and portages.

Sport and subsistence hunting also

FACING PAGE: *Kenai NWR includes part of the immense Harding Icefield, which covers the southeast side of the Kenai Peninsula. Several glaciers, including Grewingk, Tustumena, and Skilak, descend to refuge lands. (Fred Hirschmann)*

Water levels of Kenai NWR's Tustumena Lake fluctuate throughout the year. This photo was taken during spring. Tustumena, a name of Dena'ina Indian origin, is Alaska's fifth largest lake at nearly 120 square miles. (George Matz)

draw people to the refuge. While some animals can be killed year-round, seasons for premier game animals — moose, Dall sheep, and caribou — typically begin in August or September. Some areas of the refuge are closed to hunting, and some have special restrictions. As is the case with fishing, ADFG regulations apply to all hunting on this and every other Alaska refuge. Whether hunting, fishing, or just camping, firearms are allowed for bear protection in any part of the refuge. Target shooting, however, is prohibited.

Though most public use occurs in summer and fall, Kenai NWR is also a popular winter recreation destination. Snowmachining, cross-country skiing, dogsledding, and ice fishing are popular. Many Southcentral Alaska residents also take advantage of the refuge's Christmas

Range of the Giant Kenai Moose

As is sometimes the case with older national wildlife refuges, Kenai was originally established primarily for the protection of one species, the giant Kenai moose. The use of the superlative is entirely appropriate. The moose is the largest of the world's deer, and those found on the Kenai Peninsula, *Alces alces gigas*, are members of the Alaska-Yukon subspecies, largest of the world's moose.

Gigas has long been a resident of Alaska. In fact, some think the species may have arrived in the New World by way of the Bering Land Bridge. Today, moose can be encountered almost everywhere in the state, from the Southeast Panhandle to the North Slope to the sidewalks of Alaska's largest city. An adult bull in prime condition may

A cow moose and calf enter grasses and weeds several feet tall. Newborn calves weigh up to 35 pounds and within five months grow to more than 300 pounds. (Chlaus Lotscher)

stand more than seven feet high at the shoulder and weigh as much as 1,600 pounds. The antlers of the current Boone and Crockett world record, which was shot on Fortymile River in eastern Alaska, spanned more than 65 inches at their point of greatest spread.

Moose are browsers and grazers, selecting feed as the opportunity arises. In winter, their preferred browse is willow, followed by birch and aspen, though they will also dig in the snow to get to sedges, aquatic vegetation, or other buried plants. In summer their diets become more varied as nature sets a grander table. Aquatic and marsh plants become significant dietary components because moose can browse these in waters up to eight feet deep. Also common in a moose's summer menu are such forbs as fireweed and lupine. As these young plants mature and toughen, browse will again play a greater dietary role. During the summer, as much as 80 percent of a moose's waking time is spent feeding.

That changes with the rut. Breeding takes place from late September through early October. Studies have shown that bull moose on the Kenai Peninsula quit eating completely during the rut, while females reduce their feeding, but to a lesser degree. Bull moose can become quite aggressive at this time, and will engage in shoving matches, using their broad antlers, to compete for cows. Though wounds are not uncommon during these contests, the jousts seldom result in fatal injuries.

After a gestation period of approximately eight months, calves are born from mid May through early June, with a cow giving birth to one, two, or very occasionally, three calves, with quality of available forage the major factor influencing multiple births. Cows with calves are very protective, and can be dangerous. Maternal cows

Moose are often seen near the Sterling Highway in Kenai NWR. This one eats pond grasses close to the road. (Harry M. Walker)

lactate until the first autumn, at which time they wean their calves.

Moose have been important to the development of not only Kenai NWR, but the entire Kenai Peninsula and to Alaska. They've long been valuable sources of subsistence food, clothing, and tools and were once killed by market hunters to supply meat to mining camps and trophies to decorate the homes of sportsmen in the contiguous states. Today, subsistence hunters and Alaska and nonresident sport hunters kill as many as 8,000 moose a year.

Moose are an important tourist resource, too. They are far and away the big game animal most likely to be seen by summer vacationers, especially those visitors who restrict their Alaska travel to the highway system. A cluster of parked cars along the road in summer probably means a moose is nearby. ■

tree program. For the price of a short hike and a little elbow grease, they can decorate their holiday home with a black spruce.

Regardless of the season, recreation on Kenai NWR is best undertaken with preparation and a proper mental attitude. Layered clothing, survival gear, water, a first-aid kit, and food should be packed regardless of the time of year or length of trek. Hypothermia is a hazard even in midsummer, as are bear encounters, cold water crossings, and biting insects. Sudden blizzards can strand winter travelers, and avalanche awareness is essential when entering the backcountry in snow season.

Most people who visit the refuge do so by car, but daily flights are available from Homer and Anchorage, and buses run south from Anchorage. Air taxis are available to take adventurers into the refuge's roadless reaches, and approved guides or outfitters can help lead visitors to the trip of a lifetime. ■

A 1996 wildfire swept through spruce near Skilak Lake. This 2002 photo shows plant growth since then. (George Matz)

Kenai NWR: A History

The history of Kenai NWR is tied to the big game animals that inhabit its lands. The early conservation movement in the United States was sparked, to a large degree, by hunters and anglers who feared that if no action was taken to conserve the nation's fish and game future generations would only know these species in zoos and aquariums. And though Kenai NWR was established in 1941 by Franklin D. Roosevelt, its roots go far deeper, back to the turn of the century. Refuge wilderness ranger and historian Gary Titus tells the story: It all started when a wealthy big game hunter from Canon City, Colorado, traveled to Alaska in 1897, checking out rumors of giant moose on the Kenai Peninsula. Arriving in Cook Inlet, Dall DeWeese was told he would be fortunate to find a hunter by the name of Andrew Berg to guide him.

DeWeese found Berg at a Kasilof cannery and hired him. The hunt, in the Tustumena Lake region, was successful, with several trophy moose killed and the Kenai Peninsula stamped indelibly on DeWeese's mind. On the steamboat journey home DeWeese was already planning his next hunt here.

Word spread of a new territory with giant moose and white sheep, and many hunters laid plans for the season of 1898. For those lacking the time and financial wherewithal for an Alaska hunt, other means of acquiring trophies were available. At that time, there were no game regulations in Alaska, and wildlife could be openly bought and sold by anyone. Local Alaska hunters started market hunting by killing moose and caribou for their heads and selling these trophies at good prices for shipment to San Francisco and other points.

Upon DeWeese's return in the fall of 1898 he was surprised to see a marked decrease in game populations. On his southbound trip, he stopped in Sitka and voiced his concerns to the editor of the Sitka newspaper. The next day the paper's headline read, "ALASKAN GAME DOOMED. DALL DE WEESE THE GREAT HUNTER TELLS THE REASON." In this article, DeWeese made a plea for game preservation in the form of hunting laws and established game preserves.

Another big game hunter, Harry E. Lee, traveled north in the fall of 1899 to hunt the Kenai Peninsula. Lee had a good trip, yet he also saw problems developing with the lack of game laws. In a magazine article, Lee wrote, "I would like to suggest that the American sportsmen should by all means try to secure this tract of land from the Government as a game preserve, and I hope someone will take the matter in hand before another year, for the game is wantonly killed by

Photographer Tom Evans pulls a loaded canoe through a stream connecting Canoe Lakes 1 and 2 on the Swan Lake canoe system in Kenai NWR. (Jon R. Nickles)

Mountain goats inhabit mountainous areas from Southeast to the Kenai Peninsula. This group grazes slopes of the Kenai Mountains. (Chlaus Lotscher)

market hunters every winter, and if this is not soon put a stop to, it will be entirely exterminated." This call for preserving Kenai Peninsula wild game was taken up by subsequent visiting sportsmen.

Dall DeWeese returned to hunt in Alaska again in 1899 and 1901, and he continued his call for wildlife preservation. In a December 1901 letter to the new president, Theodore Roosevelt, DeWeese wrote, "This is a subject that appeals to every 'true-blue sportsman,' every lover of animal life, and all those who see beauty in nature, embracing forests, plains, and mountains throughout our entire country, and while the woods, plains, and mountains are naturally beautiful, we all agree that they are much more grand and lifelike when the wild animals and birds are present. There are now several organizations doing work toward the preservation of wild animal and bird life. There is much yet for us to do; to resolve is to act. Let us be up and at it."

Someone must have been listening, because Roosevelt's new forestry chief, Gifford Pinchot, sent a young forester named William A. Langille to reconnoiter the Kenai Peninsula in 1904. Langille traversed the peninsula from Seward to Seldovia, and during this trip he realized the unique value of the land as a wildlife and hunting preserve.

In his 1904 report, Langille opined that on the peninsula, "there is room for the frontier settler and fishermen on the shore land; there let them abide in peace and prosper, but keep out the fire and wanton game destroyers."

Langille further recommended that certain portions of the proposed Kenai Forest Reserve be specifically designated as game preserves for perpetuating the game species of the region. He recommended that Sheep Creek at the head of Kachemak Bay be set aside for Dall sheep, and that the Caribou Hills be set aside for moose and the few remaining caribou.

In 1907, following Langille's recommendations, Chugach National Forest was designated, with further additions made in 1909. At its maximum size, Chugach National Forest extended from the Copper River on the east to Cook Inlet on the west, to Kachemak Bay on the south, and included all the Chugach Mountains to the north.

Throughout the 1920s and 1930s, hunters and conservationists continued to press Congress to designate part of this land specifically as a wildlife preserve, without logging, mining, and other forms of development. Congress finally recognized these voices, and a second President Roosevelt, FDR, signed the enabling legislation for the Kenai National Moose Range on Dec. 16, 1941.

In December 1980, under ANILCA, the moose range was renamed the Kenai National Wildlife Refuge. ANILCA added almost two million acres to the refuge, designated 1.3 million acres of the new conservation area's lands as Wilderness, and expanded its purposes to include all wildlife species. ∎

Kodiak NWR

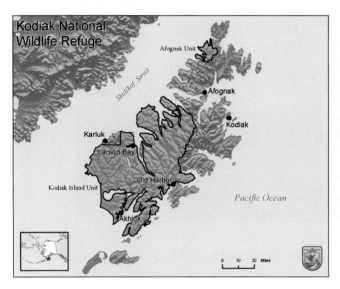

Kodiak National Wildlife Refuge

Shelikof Strait
Afognak Unit
Afognak
Kodiak
Karluk
Larson Bay
Kodiak Island Unit
Old Harbor
Pacific Ocean
Akhiok

0 10 20 Miles

Kodiak NWR

Established: 1941
Acreage: 1,923,953
Location: Two-thirds of Kodiak Island and about 50,000 acres on nearby Afognak Island

One of six mammal species introduced on Kodiak Island in the 1920s, Sitka black-tailed deer thrive here. (Tom Walker)

Founded in August 1941, when the clouds of World War II loomed over much of the planet, and just months before the United States was forced into that conflict as a result of the attack on Pearl Harbor, Kodiak NWR is proof that, even in times of great international threat and turmoil, the American people have had the wisdom and will to protect their natural treasures. Pres. Franklin D. Roosevelt's executive order creating the refuge was a result of a rising tide of conservation in the United States that dated back to the turn of the century, when sportsmen and naturalists, shaken by the extinction of the passenger pigeon and elimination of bison herds, organized to protect the nation's wild species and wild places. In fact, one of the first such organizations, the Boone and Crockett Club, was founded by Pres. Franklin D. Roosevelt's cousin, former Pres. Theodore Roosevelt, and was one of the lobbying groups that helped establish the first conservation unit on the Kodiak archipelago, the Afognak Island Forest and Fish Culture Reservation, in 1892.

The first human residents of Kodiak, the Alutiit, reached the island approximately 8,000 years ago. Prior to their arrival, during the Pleistocene, much of the archipelago was covered by ice sheets, with only the highest peaks and the southwestern portion of the island, known as the Kodiak Refugium, remaining free of ice. The refugium offered a place of refuge during this glacial period. Geologically, the island is nearly identical to the Kenai Peninsula, sharing the same rock type and structure. Geologists theorize that before the advance of glaciers, the two were connected by an unbroken chain of mountains. This link was broken approximately 12,000 years ago when Cook Inlet ice eroded the connecting rock to below sea level, isolating the islands and the species that inhabited them.

A geologic event altered Kodiak's ecosystem again on June 6, 1912, when Novarupta Volcano erupted. A trio of great explosions spread ash over Afognak and northern Kodiak. So deep was the ash that it filled lakes and had serious, if temporary, impacts on salmon spawning. The fish and the islands' vegetation recovered, and the ash may have had positive long-term effects on soil productivity.

In part because of its long isolation, the archipelago has few indigenous land mammals. In addition to the Kodiak brown bear, only red fox, river otter, short-tailed weasel, little brown bat, and tundra vole are native to the islands. In the 1920s, the Alaska Game Commission, working with local sportsmen's groups, introduced Sitka black-tailed deer, Roosevelt elk, muskrat, beaver, mountain goat, and snowshoe hare. The deer, in particular, have thrived, and draw hunters from Alaska and the rest of the United States every fall.

After the U.S. purchase of Alaska, cattle ranching and salmon fishing were among the first important industries on the islands, and when early conservation efforts caused brown bear populations to rebound, both of these were affected. Ranchers complained of increased predation on cattle in the 1930s. The commission responded by establishing a program to eliminate problem bears. A few were killed, but the commission's agents ultimately recommended against large-scale bear-control efforts, suggesting instead that the island be managed for fur, fish, and game.

During the next decade, when dwindling sockeye numbers affected the Karluk River fishery, bears were again blamed. Research revealed, however, that

98 percent of the salmon killed by bears were fish that had already successfully spawned. Once again, complaints did not result in increased bear control or liberalization of hunting seasons.

When Kodiak NWR was established in 1941, it encompassed 1,950,000 acres, including Uganik Island and large parcels on the south and west of Kodiak Island. The refuge remained unchanged through statehood. In 1971, however, ANCSA conveyed about 16 percent of Kodiak's refuge lands, or some 310,000 acres, to Native corporations. Much of this was

Kittiwakes soar above their nests on Sitkalidak Strait, near Old Harbor on Kodiak Island. Kodiak NWR encompasses most of the island and provides habitat for more than 200 bird species.
(Chlaus Lotscher)

prime Kodiak bear habitat. It took an organization established as a result of a successful environmental mitigation agreement, and one of Alaska's worse eco-disasters, to restore much of that land to the refuge.

A mountainous spine runs the length of Kodiak Island. Here, peaks rise between Kizhuyak and Terror Bays. (Fred Hirschmann)

In 1979, the Terror Lake hydroelectric project proposed construction of a dam on the refuge's Terror Lake and a tunnel through nearby mountains to carry water to a powerhouse on the Kizhuyak River. As a result of opposition to this development in prime bear habitat, a mitigation agreement was negotiated. Among other things, the agreement between USFWS and the Alaska Industrial Development Authority established the Kodiak Brown Bear Trust. Other mitigation efforts were successful, and most agree that the

hydroelectric project has had minimal impacts on Kodiak's brown bears.

Ten years later, the *Exxon Valdez* spilled 11 million gallons of oil into Prince William Sound. Driven by wind, the oil soon reached the archipelago, poisoning marine mammals and coastal birds. Though no bears were killed by the spill, the money that Exxon agreed to provide to mitigate effects of the disaster on coastal birds and marine mammals later benefited the bears and the refuge. In part through the efforts of the Kodiak Brown

Bear Trust, 290,000 acres, representing most of the refuge lands lost as a result of ANCSA conveyances, were bought back and returned to the refuge. In years since, the trust, in conjunction with sports and conservation organizations, has continued working to acquire key pieces of bear habitat.

Today, Kodiak NWR is accessible only by floatplane or boat. Spruce forests dominate the northern part of Kodiak Island and the Afognak portion of the refuge, while southern Kodiak is covered with lush, grassy hummocks. The refuge is home to many of the archipelago's approximately 3,000 brown bears and at least 500 pairs of bald eagles. Some 237 bird species live on or visit the refuge. More than 1.5 million seabirds overwinter in nearshore waters. The refuge also provides spawning and rearing habitat for five species of Pacific salmon. In fact, salmon spawned on the refuge make up approximately 65 percent of the total commercial harvest in the Kodiak archipelago.

Recreational uses of the refuge include hunting, fishing, wildlife observation, photography, rafting, and camping. The refuge also maintains several remote public-use cabins. Kodiak Island is served by commercial flights and the Alaska Marine Highway Ferry System. Air charters to the refuge are available from the town of Kodiak. ■

Kodiak Brown Bear

Perhaps as much as any other refuge in Alaska, Kodiak NWR's history has revolved around one species. Though the language of Pres. Franklin D. Roosevelt's executive order established the refuge "to preserve the natural feeding and breeding range of the brown bear *and other wildlife*," the last three words hang like an afterthought. It was the great bears that first focused the attention of conservationists on Alaska's Emerald Isle.

Because these huge bruins are the only large land mammal native to the island, they were an occasional subsistence resource for local Alutiit. Small groups of hunters pursued the bears with bows fitted with outsized arrows and defended themselves with spears if charged. Though the Alutiit relied on Kodiak bears for clothing, tools, ornamentation, and food, it is unlikely these traditional hunters had a significant impact on the population.

The Bering-Chirikov expedition made note of, but did not land on, Kodiak Island in 1741. It wasn't until 43 years later that Russian explorers first set foot on the island, followed by trappers and businessmen eager to exploit its previously untapped fur resources. Brown bear hides were not particularly prized, bringing approximately $10 apiece, but as more valuable furbearers such as sea otters became scarce, the taking of bears increased.

After the United States acquired Alaska in 1867, the commercial bear harvest continued to grow. Its impacts were soon exacerbated by cannery

A sow with two cubs fishes in Salmon Creek, which runs into Karluk Lake on the west side of Kodiak Island. Brown bear cubs are hairless at birth and weigh less than one pound. They stay with their mother for two years.
(Tom Bol Photography)

workers who, since bears were considered to be in competition with the local salmon industry, were encouraged to kill them whenever possible.

Largely because of the lobbying of sportsmen, who feared the loss of the world's largest brown bears, early harvest regulations were put into place in the 1920s. That conservation momentum led ultimately to President Roosevelt's establishment of Kodiak NWR.

This all amounts to a big role for one animal to play, but the Kodiak brown bear is worthy of the part. As are all brown bears, it is actually the same species as the grizzly bear (*Ursus arctos*), but Kodiak's bruins are a unique subspecies (*Ursus arctos middendorffi*), genetically isolated from the mainland stock of brown/grizzly bears for approximately 12,000 years.

They are, quite simply, the largest bears in the world. A fully grown boar can stand five feet high at the shoulder, and tower to 10 feet when standing on

its hind legs to get a better look at, or scent of, an intruder. A bear of that size might approach 1,500 pounds in autumn, when it would be rippling with fat in preparation for a brief, restless hibernation.

Kodiak bears typically begin denning in October. Sows that were impregnated during the May-June mating season are the first to den, with the larger boars waiting until later in the season. Some males may not hibernate at all during a given year. Boars tend to emerge from their dens earlier than sows, often venturing out in early April, while a female with winter-born cubs might remain in her den until the latter part of June.

Today, Kodiak bear hunting is regulated by ADFG. Nonresidents must hire a guide, who might charge as much as $15,000 per hunt. In a typical year, about 160 bears are taken by sport hunters on Kodiak, 70 percent of these being males. It is illegal to kill a female accompanied by cubs.

Conversely, though bear-human conflicts are not rare, human injuries occur on an average of about once every two years. And, despite the many outdoor magazine covers that have featured vicious-looking "killer bears" over the years, only one person has been killed by a Kodiak brown bear since the refuge was established.

Kodiak's bears are key to the island's economy. They bring revenue through hunting and related sporting equipment sales, air charters, and guide services and through bear viewing, which is not presently as developed as it is at other sites in Alaska such as McNeil River, but may play a more important role in the future. Tourism and services that support such visitors also generate money. Just as the founding and history of Kodiak NWR have been inextricably linked to the giant bruins, so is the future of the archipelago tied to continuing healthy populations of this greatest of the world's brown bears. ■

Koyukuk NWR

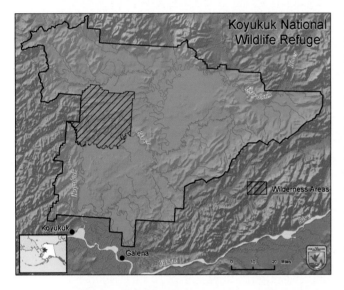

Koyukuk National Wildlife Refuge

Wilderness Areas

Koyukuk
Galena

Koyukuk NWR

Established: 1980
Acreage: 3,550,000
Designated Wilderness: 400,000 acres
Location: Floodplain of Koyukuk River north of its confluence with the Yukon in westcentral Alaska

Koyukuk NWR lies within the floodplain of the Koyukuk River in a basin surrounded by low, rolling mountains. The

Koyukuk is a tributary of the Yukon River. It flows from its source in the Brooks Range to join the Yukon at the village of Koyukuk.

Though water largely defines it, the refuge offers a range of diverse habitats and a variety of fish and wildlife that depend on it. Meandering rivers and sloughs of the floodplain are surrounded by hundreds of small lakes. Where riverbanks are high, white spruce and birch border the waters; thickets of willow and dense alders crowd banks in low-lying terrain. This brush and woodland habitat gradually gives way to open tundra slopes of surrounding mountains.

The landscapes of Koyukuk and Kaiyuh Flats (northern Innoko region) are dynamic works in progress. These are true wildlands where the ancient natural forces of fire, ice-scouring, and flood continue to shape and reshape landscape and alter courses of river systems. This constant dance of destruction and regeneration allows refuge lands to support a richness of wildlife.

Wildland fires significantly affect the uplands. In forests of the Koyukuk refuge, more than 500 lightning strikes might be recorded in a single day during June or

July. Fires ignited by these storms burn in irregular patterns and at varying intensities determined by weather, wind, and available fuels. This creates a patchwork of habitats whose vegetation is varied in species and maturity. Such variety allows the lands to meet food, water, and shelter needs of many animal species.

During spring breakup, ice assaults the lowlands. Moving sheets of it scour riverbanks and shear stands of willows on banks and sandbars. The tender new growth that results from this rough pruning provides rich pasture for moose and food for bears breaking the long fast of hibernation.

Spring rains and snowmelt periodically flood the wetlands, bringing with them a wealth of nutrients. This natural fertilizing, coupled with the effects of long, hot summer days, creates ideal conditions for growth of aquatic vegetation and invertebrates in the small, shallow lakes of the lowlands.

It is, in part, because of this combination of ice-influenced willow regeneration and flood-charged aquatic growth that the refuge's Three-Day Slough area, in the southern part of the 400,000-acre Koyukuk Wilderness, has some of the most productive moose habitat in Alaska. This region has, at times, supported more than 10 moose per square mile, and USFWS's recent counts indicate that the most productive areas still contain densities of five or more moose per square mile.

Breeding waterfowl feast on water plants and protein-rich invertebrates, and young birds grow strong quickly in the short, lush summer. As many as 100,000 ducks are hatched and raised on refuge lands during a single nesting season.

Many other species also partake of this seasonal banquet. Migratory songbirds arrive in spring from wintering grounds in Mexico and Central and South America, and refuge staff participate in spring surveys and summer bandings to determine population trends and long-term breeding success of these species. Raptors also arrive in the spring, following other feathered migrants as wolves follow a caribou migration.

In fact, caribou from the 450,000-animal Western Arctic herd often do move into the northernmost reaches of the refuge in winter months in search of lichens beneath the snow. Koyukuk NWR also supports a resident population of approximately 200 caribou in the Galena Mountain herd. Wolves, lynx, and other furbearers, as well as black and grizzly bears, are found on the refuge year-round.

Streams and rivers of the refuge complex support arctic grayling and sheefish, while northern pike, especially those that winter in the shallow lakes of the Kaiyuh Flats, sometimes grow to record size.

Residents of six nearby Alaska Native villages rely on refuge lands as a subsistence supermarket, gathering meat, fish, and berries; trapping furbearing animals for income or barter; and cutting trees for construction and firewood.

Sportfishing and hunting are permitted in accordance with state and federal regulations. All commercial activity on the refuges, including guiding and the transportation of visitors and/or gear, requires a special-use permit. Visitors should contact the refuge office before contracting any such services.

ABOVE: *Meadows and black spruce characterize Koyukuk NWR. The edge of the Nogahabara Sand Dunes can be seen at the top of photo, behind the trees. (Courtesy USFWS)*

RIGHT: *Many species of ducks migrate through Koyukuk NWR each year, including long-tailed ducks. A male is shown here. (Steven Kazlowski)*

The refuge also offers great opportunities for floating and camping. Visitors should be prepared for a true wilderness experience, however, and take reasonable

Strips of salmon caught in subsistence nets dry on racks. In combination with store-bought items, the region's Athabascan Indians use wild foods such as fish, berries, greens, and red meat. (Courtesy USFWS)

precautions, including leaving a detailed itinerary and planned date of return with friends. The upper portion of the Koyukuk River between Hughes and Huslia is popular with floaters, since large gravel bars along the wide, placid river in this stretch provide excellent wildlife viewing opportunities and campsites.

Insects can be troublesome in the summer. Camping on exposed gravel bars, away from vegetation in which these pests can rest, provides some relief, but recreationists should bring headnets, insect repellants, and even "bug jackets" to better enjoy their trip. It is a good idea to boil or chemically purify all drinking water to guard against giardiasis. ∎

Nogahabara Sand Dunes

Nestled against the Nulato Hills in Koyukuk NWR's Koyukuk Wilderness is a gift from the geologic past. The Nogahabara Sand Dunes, roughly circular in shape and six miles in diameter, look out of place among the boreal forest and arctic tundra that characterize the refuge. The dunes are an ever-shifting, wind-sculpted landscape of moving sands.

The Nogahabara, along with Kobuk Valley National Park's Great and Little Kobuk Sand Dunes, are remnants of a sheet of sand that geologists think covered the whole of the central Kobuk River Valley at the close of the Pleistocene. Moving ice and water, acting upon Alaska's bedrock, produced abundant sands, which winds then distributed over great distances. The surviving dunes are a delicate and otherworldly ecosystem, and home to a number of rare and locally rare plant species, including bugseed and an imperiled sedge. ∎

Leftover from a sheet of sand that blanketed the central Kobuk River Valley about 10,000 years ago, the Nogahabara Sand Dunes shift constantly with the wind. (Jo Overholt)

The heart of Nowitna NWR is a forested lowland basin, bisected by, and forming the floodplain of, the meandering Nowitna River. The refuge's climate is typically marked by light precipitation, mild winds, long, hard winters, and short, relatively hot, summers. Hills that circle the lowlands are capped by alpine tundra.

All but 60 of the river's 283 miles flow within the refuge. The portion of the Nowitna that drains the refuge was designated a Wild river under ANILCA. With the exception of a 15-mile section in which its waters wind through a canyon surrounded by 2,000-foot peaks, the Nowitna typically flows through flat terrain or, at most, gently rolling hills. As a result, most of the river is designated Class I (easy) water for rafters or other river travelers.

Which is not to say the Nowitna can't surprise. In the spring, for example, high water and ice dams can back it up for 100 miles or more, with resulting floods allowing fish populations to travel between usually separated lakes and sloughs. Fish species inhabiting the river and its related lakes and streams include sheefish, burbot, whitefish, sucker, king and chum salmon, northern pike, and grayling.

The meandering lower reaches of the Nowitna wander through one of Alaska's many productive waterfowl nurseries. There, the grassy margins of the river, and of other waterways that surround it, provide breeding habitat for trumpeter swans, white-fronted geese, canvasback ducks, sandhill cranes, and other migratory species. More than 120 bird

Nowitna NWR

Female American wigeons, like the one shown here, appear reddish at close range. Nowitna NWR contains habitat this species breeds in: freshwater marshes, sloughs, ponds, and marshy lake edges. (Steven Kazlowski)

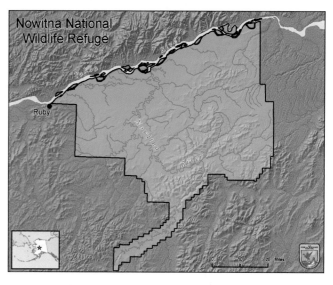

Nowitna National Wildlife Refuge

Ruby

Nowitna NWR

Established: 1980
Acreage: 1,560,000
Wild Rivers: Nowitna River
Location: 200 miles west of Fairbanks

species have been sighted on the refuge during summer, including such raptors as bald eagles, northern harriers, and rough-legged and red-tailed hawks, but only a few dozen hardy species remain through the winters.

Mature white-spruce habitat in the forested lowlands provides cover and den sites for marten, and trapping these and other furbearers remains important to the region's economy. In fact, refuge lands have been used by Athabascan Indians for

The Palisades

A seven-mile stretch of tall bluffs near the northeastern boundary of Nowitna NWR formed by the patient erosion of Yukon River waters may be among the most promising sites for paleontological research in the northern United States. Called the Palisades, or more commonly the boneyard, these cliffs, up to 300 feet high, are made up of layers of history. At river level, erosion has exposed materials deposited as long ago as three million years.

To reach signs of the more recent past, paleontologists have to scale the cliffs' banks, laboring upward and forward in time. It is not an easy climb. The walls of the Palisades are coated with glacial loess, dust ground finer than sand by the scouring of ice. The loess is perched precariously atop a substrate of sedimentary rock and coal. When dry, the loess sifts and blows and offers uncertain footing at best; when wet, it becomes a sticking, slippery goo to rival any of the famous gumbo muds of the Lower 48. Less than a foot beneath their exposed surfaces, the Palisades are locked in permafrost. This is a fine medium for preserving ancient bones but a further complication for scientists that seek them.

Rewards paleontologists have obtained for such efforts, however, have been great. As the

continuing erosion of new seasons opens additional pages of the Palisades book, a treasury of fossils and other evidence of Pleistocene animals and plants is continuously revealed. The remains of woolly mammoths poke from the loess, along with those of prehistoric bison and the ancestors of the modern horse, caribou, and moose. Less dramatic, perhaps, but of equal or greater significance, the Palisades have yielded the first remnants discovered in Alaska of the steppe lemming, a small vole now found in far northern Europe and Asia.

Fossil collecting is prohibited here for anyone other than scientists working under permit, and river travelers should remember that even moving a bone or fossil could take it out of its prehistoric context and thus lessen its value to scientists. But the world's wonders don't necessarily need to be touched to be appreciated, and a float down this section of the Yukon can offer the bonus of a glimpse into the world of 100,000 years ago, when humans had yet to set foot on the New World, and strange, great beasts still wandered a younger Yukon's shores. ∎

Plant and animal fossils have been discovered in cliffs, called the Palisades or the boneyard, along the Yukon River in Nowitna NWR. Fossil collecting here is restricted to scientists who have obtained special permits. (Leslie Kerr)

centuries for hunting, fishing, and trapping. Depending on the season, moose, wolves, lynx, wolverines, and black and grizzly bears might be encountered anywhere on the refuge.

Given the generally gentle nature of the Nowitna River, it's not surprising that float trips are a popular recreational activity. Visitors drift the river to hunt and fish, as well as simply to observe and photograph wildlife and to experience the beauty of a wild and free-flowing Alaska river.

Depending on the season, access to the refuge is possible by various means. Flying from nearby Galena is an option. Boaters can reach the refuge from Tanana or the Dalton Highway; foot, snowmachine, and dogsled access is possible from Ruby. Though most of the Nowitna is calm, water levels and currents can vary dramatically as the result of snowmelt or thunderstorms. Low summer water levels can also sometimes make floating the river both arduous and challenging. Mosquitoes can be intense during summer. ∎

One of nine new refuges established under ANILCA, Selawik NWR straddles the Arctic Circle. It could be argued that Selawik contains some of the most historically significant acreage in North America, as refuge lands once formed part of the North American portion of the Bering Land Bridge.

Recent research, notably that of the University of Colorado's Scott Elias as published in the July 4, 1996, edition of *Nature*, analyzed ancient pollen grains found in peat samples dredged from the seafloor at the presumed site of the land bridge. Using radiocarbon dating, Elias concluded that the land bridge was passable as recently as 11,000 years ago, and that its surface was probably much like the tundra found on Selawik NWR today.

In fact, tundra wetland, bordered by the Waring Mountains and Selawik Hills, is the most common habitat type found on Selawik. Estuaries, river deltas, and drier upland tundra slopes augment the wetlands. The refuge's designated Wilderness is found along its northern boundary, formed by the Waring Mountains, where refuge lands abut Kobuk Valley National Park. Sandy soil, including a patchwork habitat of sand dunes, some completely devoid of vegetation, and birch woodland mark the foothills of this area.

The refuge is home to a variety of wildlife. Thousands of caribou from the Western Arctic herd cross the refuge, while moose, grizzly bear, wolverine, and other furbearers are present year-round. Selawik's approximately 24,000 lakes provide breeding or resting habitat for

Selawik NWR

Selawik NWR's tundra wetlands support a variety of flora, including grasses, lichens, berries, willows, birches, and black spruce. (Courtesy USFWS)

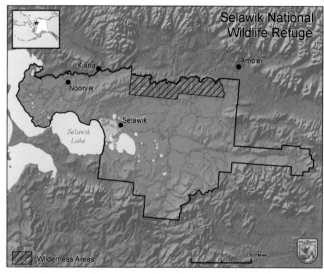

Selawik NWR

Established: 1980
Acreage: 2,150,000
Designated Wilderness: 240,000 acres
Wild and Scenic Rivers: Selawik River
Location: 360 miles northwest of Fairbanks

migratory birds, some arriving from as far away as Australia. In addition to sheefish, whitefish, grayling, and northern pike are present in the refuge's waters.

Local residents, including Inupiaq Eskimos, use refuge lands for subsistence — hunting, fishing, and gathering greens and berries. Though Selawik is difficult to get to, visitors also use refuge lands. Recreational floaters, sportfishermen, and hunters travel Selawik River in search of adventure and hunting and fishing sites. ∎

Arctic ground squirrels occur throughout most of Alaska in well-drained tundra from sea level to alpine areas. During winter, they hibernate five to eight feet underground in sleeping chambers lined with grass. (Chlaus Lotscher)

Place for Sheefish Spawning

The sheefish, or inconnu, is the largest member of the subfamily *Coregoninae*, which includes fish commonly referred to as whitefish. Sometimes called the "tarpon of the north" because of its great size, sporting nature, and its physical resemblance to the silvery, pugnacious-jawed sport fish of tropical climes, the sheefish is found only in arctic and subarctic Asia, Canada, and Alaska.

Alaska's inconnu (the name is French for "unknown," and was apparently bestowed by Hudson's Bay Company's French-Canadian voyageurs), are, like its salmon, a migratory species. Selawik NWR's sheefish hatch in the Selawik River. Biologists are uncertain where they spend their juvenile summer, though some theorize that young fish leave fresh water and move to slightly brackish Selawik Lake to feed. With the onset of winter, the river's entire population of inconnu, juveniles and adults, heads downstream to Hotham Inlet, Selawik Lake, and Kotzebue Sound and associated estuaries to escape the ice. After breakup, which can be as late as June above the Arctic Circle, the fish return to natal waters to feed and prepare for spawning, which occurs in late September and early October. Unlike salmon, sheefish can spawn many times, though adults do not necessarily reproduce every year, and are known to reach ages of more than 20 years.

The name Selawik is derived from the Inupiaq word *siilvik*, which means "place for sheefish spawning," and the population associated with the refuge is an important subsistence resource for local residents. These large fish — the Alaska record weighed 53 pounds — are also spirited

USFWS agent Frank Glaser holds two frozen sheefish caught through the ice at Kotzebue in December 1952. The larger fish weighed 40 pounds, the smaller weighed 30. (Charles Gray, courtesy USFWS)

fighters and popular with adventurous sport anglers.

Alaska's sheefish populations are, as far as biologists know, currently healthy. However, sheefish have far fewer and more localized spawning areas than salmon, a factor which could make them more vulnerable to over-harvest or habitat degradation. ∎

Tetlin NWR

Tetlin NWR embraces a dynamic landscape of snowy peaks and glacial rivers, tundra and forest and wetlands. Tetlin is nestled in a solar basin in the Upper Tanana Valley, which is typically warmer in the summer, colder in the winter, and drier than other areas in Alaska's Interior. Refuge lands are all classed as boreal forest, or taiga, and contribute to a nearly continuous band of coniferous habitat that stretches across North America and Eurasia.

As is the case in many parts of the Interior, contradictory forces of fire and flood continuously work to modify the refuge's landscape, creating a mixture of habitats dominated by varied plant species (though primarily willow and black spruce) and plant maturities. This diversity of habitat provides areas appropriate to the many species of birds, mammals, and fish that make their seasonal homes on Tetlin.

Most of the refuge's land consists of broad river basins, studded with marshes and lakes and bordered by mountains. The wide, braided Nabesna and Chisana Rivers flow north through the region and merge to form the Tanana River. The Black Hills roll across the refuge's lowlands. Farther south, the terrain rises into the foothills of the Mentasta and Nutzotin Mountains.

The Upper Tanana Valley has been called the Tetlin Passage, because it serves as a major migratory route for birds traveling to and from Canada, the Lower 48, Mexico, and South America in spring and fall. Many of these breed and nest on the refuge. Others pass through on their way to breeding and nesting grounds

Lakes and ponds dot the taiga of eastern Tetlin NWR, creating habitat for waterfowl, insects, and furbearers. (Courtesy USFWS)

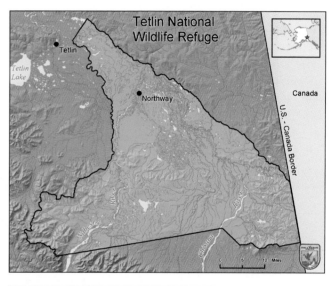

elsewhere in the Interior, on the Yukon Delta, and in the Arctic. Migrants — ducks, geese, swans, cranes, raptors, and songbirds — begin arriving in the valley in April, and continue into early June. An estimated 143 species breed on Tetlin during the short summer, when long days and warm temperatures accelerate growth of plants, aquatic insects, and other invertebrates, providing a ready

Tetlin NWR

Established: 1980
Acreage: 700,053
Location: Southwest of the Alaska Highway, bordering Canada's Yukon Territory

source of rich foods for nesting birds.

Because Tetlin is the easternmost of Alaska's mainland refuges, it supports bird species rarely found elsewhere in the

state, including red-winged blackbird and sharp-tailed grouse. The refuge is also near the western and northern habitat limits of the American coot and brown-headed cowbird.

Tetlin supports a variety of large mammals, too. Dall sheep scamper the higher slopes, while moose feed on tender growth that springs up in the wake of frequent lightning-strike fires. Wolves and grizzly and black bears range over the refuge, as do, seasonally, members of three different caribou herds. Largest of these is the 34,000-animal Nelchina herd. Two smaller herds, which are currently struggling to maintain populations, can also be found on Tetlin's lands. These are the approximately 450-member Mentasta

The Chisana River flows northwest through Tetlin NWR near the Alaska Highway. Its name is from an Athabascan Indian word meaning "red river." (Harry M. Walker)

herd and the even smaller Chisana herd. The demise of the latter is of special concern as some biologists consider these animals to be woodland caribou (*Rangifer tarandus caribou*). If this is the case, they would be the only examples of this subspecies found in Alaska, where barrenground, or Grant's, caribou (*Rangifer tarandus grantus*) are the norm.

Two of Alaska's six known humpback whitefish spawning areas in the Yukon River drainage are located within Tetlin, and along with caribou and moose, these fish are important subsistence resources for area residents. Grayling, northern pike, and lake trout are also common in the refuge's many streams and lakes.

Because it is one of only two road-accessible refuges in Alaska, Tetlin offers ample recreational opportunities. Its northern border extends 65 miles along the Alaska Highway. A visitor center, seven scenic pullouts, two lakefront campgrounds, and two established and maintained trails are available to those who want to enjoy the refuge without wandering too far afield. Backcountry hiking, canoeing, fishing, and hunting invite the more adventurous. Access to the interior of the refuge is limited to canoes, river boats, snow machines, and small aircraft fitted with floats in summer or skis in winter. Charter air services into the refuge are available out of Tok. ∎

Trumpeter Swans

The world's largest swan, with males averaging 28 pounds, the trumpeter once bred across a wide territory from the Bering Sea east though most of Canada and south to Missouri, Illinois, and Indiana. Coveted for their snowy plumage and meat, the huge birds were favorite targets of market hunters around the turn of the last century. In fact, by the early 1900s they had been hunted to near extinction. It's likely that only passage of the landmark Migratory Bird Treaty Act in 1918 saved this species. By 1932, the best estimates of the swan's world population stood at less than 70 birds breeding in the vicinity of Yellowstone Park. To better protect this remnant group's breeding ground, Red Rock Lakes NWR was established in 1935. Early recovery efforts consisted primarily of reintroducing birds from this protected population onto other refuges in the Midwest.

Then, in the early 1950s, a previously unidentified breeding population of trumpeter swans was discovered in Alaska. The first comprehensive aerial survey of these birds was conducted in 1968, when USFWS staff counted 2,847 trumpeters. This discovery calmed fears that the swans were on the verge of extinction, although they are still classified as rare or endangered in some states. The Alaska population thrived in the latter half of the twentieth century. The most recent census, in 2000, found 17,155 of these majestic birds in Alaska, accounting for more than 70 percent of the world's population.

Probably expanding their range as a result of increasing numbers, trumpeter swans were first observed breeding on Tetlin NWR in 1982. The refuge's population, centered in the Upper Tanana Valley, has grown dramatically in the years since, from 44 adults in 1982 to 934 in 2000. Today, a drive along the eastern end of the Alaska Highway in autumn, when the refuge's many migratory birds prepare to fly south, provides perhaps one of the public's best opportunities to view this species that beat the odds. ∎

Trumpeter swans, a species whose population in eastern Alaska is growing, are often seen from the Alaska Highway. Tetlin NWR wetlands are a haven for migratory birds. (Roy Corral)

Road travelers can stop at Tetlin NWR visitor center, 40 miles from the Alaska / Canada border, to learn about the refuge's plants, animals, and people. (Bob Butterfield)

Togiak NWR

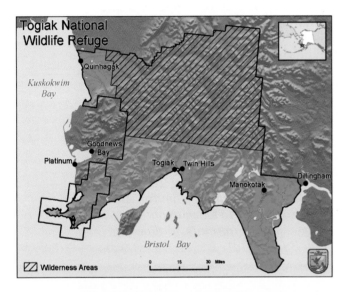

Togiak National Wildlife Refuge

Kuskokwim Bay

Quinhagak

Goodnews Bay

Platinum

Togiak Twin Hills

Manokotak

Dillingham

Bristol Bay

0   15   30 Miles

Wilderness Areas

Togiak NWR

Established: 1969
Acreage: 4,098,391
Designated Wilderness: 2,270,799 acres
Location: Between the Kuskokwim River and Bristol Bay in southwestern Alaska

Dominated by the Ahklun Mountains in the north and the cold waters of Bristol Bay to the south, Togiak NWR presents the traveler with a kaleidoscope of landscapes.

Craggy peaks, tumbling rapids and meandering braided rivers, lakes approaching 1,000 feet deep, rolling tundra, ponds, estuaries, coastal lagoons, wave-pounded cliffs, and tidal extremes among the highest on Earth characterize the refuge.

The natural forces that have shaped this landscape range from the violent and powerful to the geologically patient. Earthquakes and volcanoes filled the former role, and their marks can still be found, but it was the gradual advance and retreat of Pleistocene ice that carved many of Togiak's physical features. Some 35,000 years ago, and again only 15,000 years ago, ice sheets advanced onto the lands that make up Togiak today. When the ice retreated, it left deep glacial cirques; strange, split-level hanging valleys; and the gravelly fingers of moraines. The glaciers gouged new lakebeds more than 900 feet deep into bedrock, and in an unusual combination of the dramatic and the patient, a volcanic eruption that took place under the glacial ice formed a rare flat-topped volcano, or *tuya*, near the present-day village of Twin Hills.

Though probably not predating the last ice age, Togiak NWR's human history is venerable as well. Archaeological evidence at a site in Security Cove, near Cape Newenham, suggests humans might have inhabited that area as much as 5,000 years ago, and other research indicates some sites within the refuge have been continuously occupied for at least 2,000 years. Historically, three separate groups of people have lived within the refuge borders: The Kuskowogamiut Eskimos in the area from the Kuskokwim River south to Chagvan Bay, the Togiagamiut Eskimos from Nanvak Bay east to Cape Constantine, and the Alegemiut Eskimos of the Nushagak Bay area.

Research indicates that Native peoples of southwestern Alaska first encountered European culture when Capt. James Cook's expedition reached Cape Newenham on July 16, 1778. One hundred and two years later, the 1880 census counted more than 2,300 people in the area that now makes up the Togiak refuge. The region's rich resources, including terrestrial and marine mammals and fresh- and saltwater fish, supported population concentrations that could not have survived in many areas of Alaska.

The fur trade was probably the area's first commercial economy. Russia established Aleksandrovski Redoubt at Nushagak in 1818, and the fort was soon handling as many as 4,000 pelts a year. After the United States's purchase of Alaska from Russia, the first salmon canneries were established in Bristol Bay in 1884, and commercial fishing supplanted trapping as the region's most important industry. Gold, so important to the development of Alaska, was briefly important to the Togiak region, too. A discovery near Goodnews Bay in 1900 lured miners from

Nome, and placer mines operated in the area until the middle of the century.

Reindeer herding is yet another industry that has contributed to the economy of the region. These animals were introduced to Togiak, Nushagak, Goodnews, and Quinhagak in the early 1900s, and herding continued to be important until a series of hard winters wiped out most of the reindeer by the 1940s. The discovery of platinum in the Salmon River Valley in 1926 sparked a stampede, and mining for this metal continued until 1975, with some 640,000 ounces extracted from the Goodnews Bay district.

Of all these industries, fishing has maintained its economic importance to the region. However, with establishment of Cape Newenham NWR in 1969 and its expansion into Togiak NWR in 1980, attention turned to the recreational and scientific values of other natural resources supported by this rich ecosystem.

Refuge lands and waters support 48 mammal species, 31 of which are terrestrial and 17 marine. More than 150,000 caribou from three herds — Kilbuck, Nushagak Peninsula, and Mulchatna — use refuge lands, which they share with wolves, moose, brown and black bears, wolverines, red foxes, marmots, beavers, and porcupines. Seals, sea lions, walrus, and whales are found in season along the refuge's 600 miles of coastline.

Some 201 species of birds have been sighted on the refuge. Among them are the threatened Steller's eider, several arctic goose species, common and thick-billed murres, horned and tufted puffins, black- and red-legged kittiwakes, and various seabirds, waterfowl, shorebirds, songbirds,

ABOVE: *Cape Newenham, now part of Togiak NWR, was one of Capt. James Cook's stops during his voyage of 1778. (Courtesy USFWS)*

RIGHT: *A natural sea arch forms at Cape Peirce, which juts into the Bering Sea about 25 miles west of Hagemeister Island. The cape was named in 1869 for Benjamin Peirce, superintendent of the Coast Survey. (Fred Hirschmann)*

and raptors. Refuge staff have also documented more than 500 species of plants, demonstrating a high degree of biodiversity for a subarctic area.

Togiak NWR is blessed with abundant water. With 1,500 miles of stream and river habitat in 35 river systems, and 25 lakes larger than 400 acres, as well as Bristol Bay, the refuge provides habitat for 33 species of fish, including the more than one million Pacific salmon, of the five North American species, that return to the refuge to spawn each year.

It should be no surprise, then, that some of the finest remote sportfishing in the

world can be found along the Kanektok, Goodnews, and Togiak Rivers. Hunting for large and small game is also popular, and guided and unguided hunts are available. Togiak refuge also boasts the second largest contiguous Wilderness area in the national wildlife refuge system. The nearly 2.3-million-acre Togiak Wilderness attracts floaters and backpackers who come to hunt and fish or simply to observe and photograph the wildlife and spectacular scenery. Access to the refuge is primarily by bush plane or boat. There are no roads, trails, or campgrounds anywhere on the refuge, so visitors should come prepared for a truly wild experience. ∎

Pacific Walrus

Each year, from spring to autumn, waters of Bristol and Kuskokwim Bays host sizable numbers of Pacific walrus. The walruses summering in Bristol Bay are predominately adult males. These bachelors migrate north in the fall to join the rest of the population, which overwinters in polynyas, areas of open water, south of St. Lawrence Island, Nunivak Island, and in Russia's Gulf of Anadyr.

Bristol Bay walruses spend the summer feeding on benthic invertebrates and resting at isolated coastal haulouts around the bay. Two of the most used haulouts, Cape Peirce and Cape Newenham, are within Togiak NWR. There are only two other frequently used land haulouts in North America. During summer, the refuge operates a walrus haul-out monitoring and visitor program. Staff biologists daily count walruses at the haulouts, document incidences of walrus disturbance, and support other marine mammal researchers. These studies are important because, although its distinctive appearance and role in stories and songs have made the walrus one of the most recognizable of arctic animals, there is much about these marine mammals that scientists do not know.

The Pacific walrus population is a valuable resource to coastal Natives in Alaska and Russia's Chukotka region. For thousands of years, walrus hunting has been an important source of food and raw materials for traditional equipment and handicrafts. In Alaska, Yupik-speaking Natives refer to walruses as *asveq, kaugpak,* or *ayveq*. To Inupiaq speakers the walrus is *aivik* and, to Aleut speakers, *amak* or *amaghak*. Native languages include many additional terms for walruses of specific ages, sexes, and body conditions.

Pacific walrus are one of the largest species of pinnipeds, web-footed marine mammals, in the Northern Hemisphere. The genus name, *Odobenus,* translates as "tooth walker," referring to the fact that walrus use their tusks to drag themselves onto, and move on, land or ice. Adult males can weigh more than 3,600 pounds, exceed 10 feet in length, and are approximately 45 percent heavier and 18 percent longer than females. The distinctive tusks are true teeth, like those of elephants. In addition to their usefulness in moving the huge animals around when out of the water, tusks are used in courtship and threat displays and as weapons of defense. The tusks of male walruses are generally larger than those of

Walruses rest on a rocky shore. Skilled Alaska Native carvers use walrus ivory for sculptures, masks, and jewelry. (Robin Brandt)

females. A big bull might show as much as 30 inches of ivory.

Walruses are generally found in waters of 325 feet or less, possibly because of higher food productivity in this relatively shallow water. Feeding areas are typically composed of sediments of soft, fine sands or rocky substrates; compacted sediments apparently inhibit foraging. Walruses can ingest as many as 6,000 prey items in a single feeding session. Bivalve mollusks, such as clams, are their most common food; however, other invertebrates, including sea cucumbers, crabs, and segmented worms, are also eaten. Some walrus even eat seals.

Walruses use their sensitive vibrissae to locate prey in the sediments of the seafloor. With head down and vibrissae in contact with the bottom, they propel themselves forward by sculling with their hind flippers. They use their nose, jets of water, and suction to dislodge prey from the sediments. This intensive tilling of the seafloor is thought to have a profound influence on the ecology of the Bering Sea. The foraging activity of walruses recycles large quantities of nutrients from the seafloor back into the water column, providing food for scavenger organisms, and thus contributing to the health and diversity of the benthic community.

Researchers have long found it interesting that the stomachs of walrus feeding on clams seldom contain shell fragments. They have speculated that the animals crush the clams in their mouths and spit out the shells, or even that they smash them between front flippers and let the heavy shells drift to the bottom while slurping up the suspended meat. The current theory, first proposed in 1950, is that walrus literally suck the clams out of their shells. Here's how the late Francis W. "Bud" Fay, dean of modern U.S. walrus researchers, de-

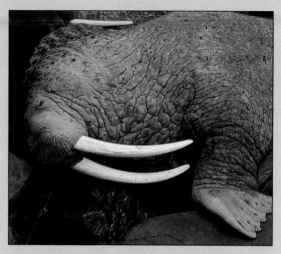

The thick skin of the Pacific walrus allows it to sleep comfortably atop jagged rocks. Skin color varies in response to changes in air or water temperature. (Daryl Pederson)

scribes an attempt to test this hypothesis: "In June, 1958 I was present in the New York Aquarium at a regular feeding of Olaf, a three-year-old male walrus that had been in captivity since infancy. At the time of my visit, his daily ration consisted entirely of soft-shelled clams ... that were prepared for him only by removal of the shells. I selected one of the largest of those shell-free clams; holding it firmly in my fist with only the siphon exposed, I offered it to the walrus. He took my fist in his lips and, in an instant, removed the siphon by suction and swallowed it, leaving the remainder of the clam still in my hand." It seems Fay was confident the shell-crushing theory was not viable.

A walrus's color changes in response to temperature. When in cold water, walrus are drab, varying from brownish-gray to dull yellow. On land or ice, particularly on a warm or sunny day, they may turn darker brown or even pink. The change is visual evidence of the animal's ability to regulate its body temperature. In a cold environment, a walrus concentrates its blood around its body core to conserve heat. When the animal becomes warm, its blood vessels dilate, sending blood closer to the surface of the skin where it can radiate away excess heat.

Based on records of the large sustained harvests in the eighteenth and nineteenth centuries, scientists think the Pacific walrus population included at least 200,000 animals prior to the onset of commercial hunting. Since then, population size has fluctuated markedly in response to varying levels of human exploitation. Large-scale commercial harvests reduced the population to an estimated 50,000 to 100,000 animals in the mid 1950s. This number increased rapidly during the 1960s and 1970s as a result of reductions in hunting pressure. Between 1975 and 1990, aerial surveys were carried out by the United States and Russia at five-year intervals, producing population estimates ranging from 201,039 to 234,020. Efforts to survey the Pacific walrus population were suspended after 1990 due to unresolved problems with survey methods that produced unreliable population estimates. The current size of the Pacific walrus population is unknown.

Recently, new tools, including thermal sensing technology that can locate walruses by their body heat and high-definition satellite imagery, have shown potential for helping scientists better understand the size and distribution of the Pacific walrus population. These tools and the steady accumulation of other evidence will help researchers better understand and appreciate these most interesting citizens of Togiak NWR. ■

Yukon Delta NWR

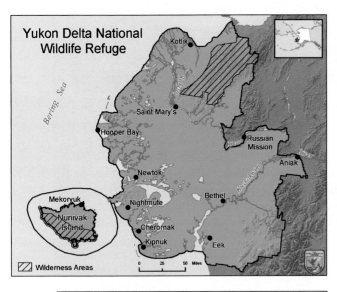

Yukon Delta National Wildlife Refuge

- Kotlik
- Saint Mary's
- Hooper Bay
- Russian Mission
- Newtok
- Aniak
- Mekoryuk
- Nunivak Island
- Nightmute
- Bethel
- Chefornak
- Kipnuk
- Eek

Bering Sea

Wilderness Areas   0   25   50 Miles

Yukon Delta NWR

Established: 1909
Acreage: 19,166,094
Designated Wilderness: 1,900,000 acres
Wild and Scenic Rivers: Andreafsky River
Location: Deltas of the Yukon and
Kuskokwim Rivers and associated
coastal wetlands along the Bering Sea

Portions of Yukon Delta NWR were first set aside by Pres. Theodore Roosevelt as the Yukon Delta Reservation, one of 51

Two miles downstream from Marshall, on the Yukon River, residents construct a fence of willows as a fish trap. (Paul D. Adams, courtesy USFWS)

federal bird reservations established during his presidency. Today's refuge, incorporating the previously established Clarence Rhode, Nunivak, and Hazen Bay refuges, was consolidated in 1980 under ANILCA, and is, after Arctic NWR, the second largest in the national wildlife refuge system. Here, waters of the Yukon and Kuskokwim Rivers flow through an immense tundra-covered wetland. Almost

70 percent of the refuge is below 100 feet elevation, and consists of a broad, flat delta stitched with rivers and streams and dotted with countless lakes, sloughs, and ponds. In fact, a third of Yukon Delta NWR is covered in water. Bordering the flat expanse are 2.5 million acres of forest and shrub habitat and uplands sporting mountains more than 4,000 feet high.

Proving the wisdom of its selection as a federal bird reservation, the refuge's varied habitats support millions of migrating raptors, songbirds, seabirds, shorebirds, and waterfowl. In terms of density and species diversity, the Yukon Delta is the most important shorebird nesting area in the United States. Birds from six major flyways, from the Atlantic Ocean to the east coast of Asia, nest on the refuge or stop to rest and feed on their way to more distant nesting grounds. Almost the entire world populations of bristle-thighed curlews and black turnstones breed on the refuge, which also hosts more than a million ducks and half a million geese every year. Two of the seaducks that visit the delta, the spectacled and Steller's eiders, are listed as threatened and are protected under the Endangered Species Act.

The Yukon and Kuskokwim Rivers and their tributaries provide hundreds of miles of spawning and rearing habitat for fish. A total of 44 species use the refuge's fresh and marine waters, including five Pacific salmon, Dolly Varden, northern pike, sheefish, grayling, several species of whitefish, burbot, and rainbow trout.

The drier upland habitats boast populations of grizzly and black bears, caribou from the Western Arctic and

Mulchatna herds, moose, and wolves. Offshore, Nunivak Island supports a herd of muskox. Along the coast, waters of the Bering Sea support a variety of marine mammals, including harbor, ribbon, and bearded seals, and walrus. Several species of whales migrate along the refuge's coast. For centuries this abundance of wildlife has placed the Yukon Delta at the heart of Yup'ik Eskimo culture in Alaska. More than 40 Yup'ik villages are located within the refuge, none of which are accessible by road. A traditional subsistence hunting and fishing lifestyle is still practiced by most residents, with fish making up as much as 75 percent of the yearly food supply in many delta villages. Bethel, one

ABOVE: *Surface travel across the Yukon Delta is almost impossible except during winter, when snow and ice cover the marshy ground. (Roy Corral)*

RIGHT: *A Central Yup'ik woman fishes for tomcod in Yukon Delta NWR. Subsistence is practiced widely throughout the delta. (Courtesy USFWS)*

of the largest communities in Western Alaska, lies within Yukon Delta and serves as a transportation and supply hub for surrounding villages.

Access to the refuge is primarily by charter aircraft, and excellent hunting,

fishing, and backcountry recreation opportunities exist. Visitors should keep in mind that winter begins in October on the delta, and that insects are abundant in summer. A safe trip depends on careful planning. The refuge's visitor center in Bethel can help travelers select local charter flights and outfitters when planning a trip. ∎

Nunivak Island

Before ANILCA incorporated Nunivak Island into Yukon Delta NWR, the island was itself a conservation unit. It was set aside by Pres. Herbert Hoover in April 1929, as the Nunivak Island Reservation.

At approximately 1.5 million acres, Nunivak lies in the Bering Sea about 18 miles off the Yukon-Kuskokwim Delta coast. It is a volcanic island, covered by tundra that often rests directly atop ancient lava. In the island's interior, exposed lava flows and explosion craters, some of which contain deep lakes, further support Nunivak's fiery geological history. A plateau with peaks reaching to 1,600 feet is drained by more than 40 rivers, many of which feed into saltwater lagoons backed by sand dunes.

Each year the island hosts great numbers of migratory birds, waterfowl pausing during migration to forage on eelgrass growing in estuaries and seabirds that nest on coastal cliffs. Nunivak's relatively few predators, red and arctic fox, mink, and short-tailed weasels, and the great number of fish in its nearshore waters make a productive rookery for 14 species of seabirds including cormorants, puffins, auklets, and gulls. Nunivak once had wolves, but they were killed off by the middle of the twentieth century.

Seals, Steller sea lions, and walrus can be found seasonally along the coast. Occasionally, orcas and beluga whales are seen. Caribou once roamed Nunivak's uplands, but they disappeared before 1900.

All North American species of Pacific salmon, as well as Dolly Varden, spawn in Nunivak's rivers. Healthy populations of Pacific cod, halibut, and other species swim offshore.

This wealth of subsistence resources has supported human life on the island for more than 2,500 years. In fact, Bureau of Indian Affairs researchers have excavated materials from the island radio-carbon dated to at least 670 B.C. Nunivak's Native population, who call themselves *Nunivarmiut*, or "people of Nunivak," used all of the island's resources, weaving nets to catch fish, primarily cod, and seals, and rappelling down cliff faces on ropes of seal or walrus skin to collect seabird eggs.

Additional resources became available to them when two of the original aims of the Nunivak Island Reservation were fulfilled. In 1935, a small group of muskox from Greenland were imported to the United States to reestablish an Alaska population extirpated in the mid 1800s. The animals were kept at Fairbanks for five years for study, then 31 were sent to Nunivak to establish a herd. As this herd grew, individuals were transplanted to Nelson Island, the Seward Peninsula, the Alaska Arctic, and to Russia. Today, Oomingmak, the Musk Ox

Producers' Co-operative, owned by about 250 Yup'ik and Inupiaq women, buys *qiviut*, the under-wool of the muskox, to have it spun into yarn and distributed to knitters for scarves, hats, tunics, and other garments. Income from sales adds to the mixed cash-subsistence economy of Western Alaska.

Reindeer had been introduced to the island in 1920. These animals were later interbred with caribou from Mount McKinley National Park and the resulting animals, bigger and more difficult to herd than their domestic forebears, have thrived. Today reindeer herding and harvesting of subsistence resources supports many of the island's Native residents.

Although reindeer herding and subsistence activities do occur over most of the island, Nunivak is still largely a place of wildness and solitude. Congress designated most of southern Nunivak, approximately 600,000 acres, as Wilderness when the island was incorporated into the Yukon Delta refuge.

A number of tour and guide services, all based in Mekoryuk, the island's population center, specialize in Nunivak adventures. Information on these outfitters is available from the staff of Yukon Delta NWR. ∎

LEFT: *Reindeer mill around a pen in Mekoryuk, on Nunivak Island. The species was introduced here in 1920. (Dave Cline, courtesy USFWS)*

RIGHT: *Vegetation nearly covers the Oongalambingoi Dunes on the southeastern coast of Nunivak Island. (Courtesy USFWS)*

The Yukon Flats, a broad wetland plain drained by 300 miles of the Yukon River and bounded to the north and south by the Brooks Range and the White Mountains respectively, has been called the most productive arctic wildlife habitat in North America. Shaped over the centuries by water and ice of the meandering Yukon, this vast valley is a natural and undisturbed ecosystem.

As is the case with most rich habitats, Yukon Flats NWR is a place of water. Ten major waterways and countless streams wander over its floodplain before adding their flows to the Yukon River. As many as 20,000 lakes, ponds, and wetlands add diversity to the refuge's watery habitat. In typical interior Alaska fashion, lightning-sparked fires — as many as 2,000 strikes a day produce the highest incidence of naturally occurring wildfires in Alaska — join with floods to create a succession of terrestrial habitats, featuring vegetation of varying types and ages, which, in turn, create habitat for a diversity of species.

A variety of aquatic plant life also thrives as the shallow lakes warm under the sunshine of the short, hot summer. Bulrush, cattail, pondweed, sedges, and other water-loving plants support huge populations of insects and other invertebrates, all of which provide a bountiful table for various species of wildlife.

The third largest conservation area in the refuge system, Yukon Flats supports the highest density of breeding ducks in Alaska, and is one of the most productive waterfowl nurseries in North America. These visitors begin to arrive before ice on the Yukon breaks up in May, pausing to rest and feed in the smaller ponds that

experience the earliest ice-out before continuing their migrations north. Later migrants arrive in millions to summer on the flats. Waterfowl banded on the refuge have been recovered in Belize, Columbia, Costa Rica, the Dominican Republic, El Salvador, Guatemala, Honduras, Mexico, Panama, and Russia, as well as in eight Canadian provinces and 45 U.S. states. These birds include as much as 20 percent of the North American population of canvasbacks, up to 18,000 loons (including common, Pacific, and red-throated), 5,000 Canada geese, and 6,000 white-fronted geese. Though waterbirds and shorebirds make up the bulk of the refuge's summer avian population, more than 150 species of birds use the flats, and a songbird banding station once operated on the refuge had the highest capture rate of any in Alaska.

Most of Yukon Flats's birds are temporary residents, fleeing south before winter closes over the land. Thirteen species, however, including boreal chickadees, great gray owls, spruce grouse, three-toed woodpeckers, and ravens, remain on the refuge year-round.

The same landscape that so favors waterfowl is also beneficial to furbearers, many of which, including mink, beaver,

Yukon Flats NWR

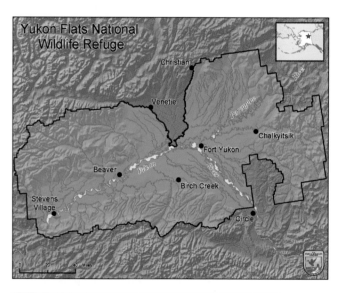

Yukon Flats National Wildlife Refuge

Christian

Venetie

Chalkyitsik

Fort Yukon

Beaver

Birch Creek

Stevens Village

Circle

Yukon Flats NWR

Established: 1980
Acreage: 8,630,319
Wild and Scenic Rivers: Beaver Creek
Location: 100 miles north of Fairbanks

muskrat, and river otter, thrive here. Moose also benefit from new growth encouraged by fire and flood, and can be found throughout the refuge. These large ungulates are the region's most important game animal; for many subsistence hunters living on or around the refuge, "moose" is synonymous with "meat."

Grizzly bears are found throughout the refuge in low concentrations, while the more common black bears tend to keep to forested lowlands. Wolves can also be encountered anywhere on the flats. These predators benefit from the fact that two of Alaska's caribou herds use Yukon Flats NWR: The more than 120,000-member Porcupine herd ranges through the northeastern portion of the refuge for part of the year, while the much smaller

BELOW: *Ice-wedge polygons, created by contraction and expansion of permafrost throughout the seasons, are areas of ground bordered by straight, ice-filled cracks. These were photographed in Yukon Flats NWR. (Jo Goldmann, courtesy USFWS)*

RIGHT: *About 600 people live at Fort Yukon, at the confluence of the Yukon and Porcupine Rivers. The area is one of the best places in Alaska during winter to view the aurora borealis. (Courtesy USFWS)*

(approximately 700-animal) White Mountain herd forages along the southern boundary of the refuge. Dall sheep can be found on alpine tundra of the White Mountains and Brooks Range.

Given the refuge's wealth of rivers, streams, lakes, and ponds, it's not surprising that fish are an important component of this ecosystem. The three species of salmon that pass through the refuge — chum, chinook, and coho — travel farther from the sea than do the salmon of any other river system in the world. Of these, chum, as well as migratory sheefish, have important spawning areas within the refuge. Resident fish include burbot, grayling, pike, and several species of whitefish.

Archaeologists think, based upon evidence found in the region, that the Yukon Flats formed part of the route by which Siberian hunters, after crossing the Bering Land Bridge, entered North America more than 10,000 years ago. Today's resident Native Americans are Gwitch'in and Koyukon Athabascan, related to the Navajo and Apache tribes of the U.S. Southwest.

The fur trade first lured people of European descent into Yukon Flats. When John Bell of the Hudson's Bay Company floated the Porcupine River to the flats in 1845, he recognized the wealth to be had in the region's relatively untapped populations of furbearers. Two years later Fort Yukon was established at the confluence of the Porcupine and Yukon. It was one of

Canvasback Ducks

When Yukon Flats NWR was established in 1980, waterfowl hunters and wildlife enthusiasts were concerned about the status of the canvasback duck. Largest of the pochards, a group of diving ducks, the canvasback was in the middle of a long population decline.

Before passage of the 1918 Migratory Bird Treaty Act, canvasbacks, considered by many to be among the most delicious of waterfowl, had been favored targets of market hunters. Because these large ducks tend to congregate in flocks in open water, they were especially susceptible to "punt" gunners of the Lower 48, whose over-sized, cannonlike shotguns or multiple-barreled battery guns, could kill dozens of the birds with a single shot. With establishment of a regulated waterfowl harvest, canvasbacks recovered only to face another dramatic population crash in the late 1980s and early 1990s. This second decline is thought to have resulted from loss of breeding and wintering habitat. Many of the prairie potholes favored by this and other species of waterfowl have been filled or drained, allowing drought years to more greatly impact their populations. A second factor is poisoning from ingesting lead shot, a threat that should diminish as more waterfowl hunters obey recent lead shot bans.

There is evidence that as habitat is lost elsewhere, the Yukon Flats, where more than 70 percent of Alaska's canvasbacks nest, could become even more important to the species. Researchers estimate that between 10 and 15 percent of the U.S. canvasback population cur-

Canvasbacks have black bills, but only the males exhibit a dark reddish head. The species can be distinguished from other ducks by its sloping forehead. (Tom Soucek)

rently nests on the refuge, a percentage that seems to be gradually increasing. Furthermore, when drought hits prairie breeding areas, as it did in 2000 and 2002, the number of canvasbacks that migrate to Alaska increases dramatically, by 119 percent in 2000 and 63 percent in 2002.

Despite recent declines, in late 2002 the canvasback population was estimated to be 600,000 birds. But history has seen these flocks boom and bust, and if drought conditions persist in the prairies, the "prince of waterfowl" will probably continue to look north for relief. ■

Neil Rome of Girdwood, near Anchorage, tends camp along the Yukon River. Rome and friend John Woodbury spent a leisurely 33 days floating the river between Eagle and the Dalton Highway in June and July 1992. (John Woodbury)

the first English-speaking communities in Alaska and, by the 1920s, the most important fur collection point in the territory. Today, trapping, hunting, and fishing are still vital to the economies of the seven villages that lie within or adjacent to the refuge.

Visitors, too, come to Yukon Flats to hunt and fish. Other recreational activities, most of which involve river floating as a means of travel, include camping, hiking, and wildlife observation and photography. Visitors can expect to find a land of extremes, with one of the widest temperature ranges in North America. Lows in excess of minus 70 degrees Fahrenheit have been recorded, and that figure does not take wind chill into account; conversely, Fort Yukon holds the high-temperature record for Alaska at 100 degrees. There are no developed campsites or trails on the refuge. Like many of its sister conservation lands in Alaska, it offers the well-prepared backcountry traveler the chance to experience an area shaped by nature, not by human activity. ■

Present Imperfect: Challenges Facing Alaska's Refuges

Twenty-five years ago, on the eve of ANILCA and the 75th anniversary of the national wildlife refuge system, Christine Enright of USFWS's Division of National Wildlife Refuges said, "During the next two years, some 40 to 50 million acres of ... remarkable wildlife habitat may be added to the national wildlife refuge system, more than doubling its present size. This is not old farm land in need of restoration, the last '40' of hardwoods in the county, or just six more potholes. On the larger new units we are talking about acquiring whole ecosystems with their watersheds intact, their rivers and

streams clear and pure, and their wildlife populations healthy and complete.

"... In acquiring this land, we will be making commitments to maintain the ecological integrity and environmental quality of the habitat and acres in our charge. We will also be accountable for maintaining optimum levels of species populations in all of their natural diversity."

Today, most people's vision of Alaska's national wildlife refuges would match Enright's description of vast, untouched places. For most refuge land in the state, this vision is an accurate one. Even here in Alaska, however, a few refuges face challenges. In some places, contaminants linger in refuge soils and waters. In others, pressures urging development require careful balancing of today's needs against the rights of future generations to inherit lands as pristine as they are under current management.

Kenai NWR: Coping With Contamination

The nearly two-million-acre Kenai NWR is the most visited of Alaska's refuges due to easy access via the road system and abundant salmon and other sport fish that lure anglers. Despite heavy use, most of the Kenai refuge is pristine, and 1.35 million acres is designated Wilderness.

Throughout the years prior to and since its original establishment as the Kenai National Moose Range, however, portions of this refuge have been exposed to a variety of contaminants. In an attempt to understand the scope and severity of this problem, USFWS began a contaminant assessment study in 1999, the results of which were published in 2001. The study identified a number of contaminants that had been introduced onto the refuge.

Primary sources of contamination are related to oil and gas development. Facilities are in operation today at Swanson River Field, established in 1956, and Beaver Creek Field, established in 1967. Throughout the years these two facilities have been responsible for hundreds of spills and other contamination events, ranging from a two-gallon spill of corrosion inhibitor to a spill of almost 239,000 gallons of highly saline "produced water,"

FAR LEFT: *Dressed in protective clothing, workers check soil for PCBs at the Swanson River oil and gas field. Toxic chemicals leaked into the area after a 1972 explosion at the field's main compressor plant. Detected years later, clean-up efforts followed. Exploratory drilling here in 1957 sparked the industry's boom in Alaska. (Bob Richey, courtesy USFWS)*

FACING PAGE: *Scott Stolnack walks his boat through vegetation at the edge of a lake on Kenai NWR's Swan Lake canoe route. (Fred Hirschmann)*

This aerial view looks southwest over wetlands near Kinzaroff Lagoon at the head of Cold Bay. (Courtesy USFWS)

use. USFWS hopes to conduct additional studies to investigate other possibly contaminated sites, and to determine how successful cleanup efforts have been at known sites. Biologists also plan to initiate studies of a variety of wildlife species that use the refuge, including resident and anadromous/migratory species, to determine baseline levels of contamination in these populations.

Officials hope the studies, coupled with a better-supported contaminant assessment and monitoring program on operating oil and gas fields, will help the refuge prevent future contamination and continue to clean up problems of the past.

Izembek NWR: A Road Through Wilderness?

Although the move to build a 33.5-mile road across portions of the Izembek Wilderness to connect the communities of King Cove and Cold Bay, providing safe, year-round access between the two settlements, dates back at least 20 years, it came to a head in 1998.

None of the parties involved (including the Aleutians East Borough, the City of King Cove, the King Cove Corp. and the Alaska congressional delegation on one side and the Department of the Interior and the White House on the other) questioned that residents of King Cove were justified in their concerns. Locals could only reach the all-weather airport at Cold Bay by boat or small plane; such travel can be dangerous, particularly in bad weather, and help could seem desperately far away to someone in need of emergency medical care.

The Department of the Interior, however, objected to the project because

a drilling byproduct. Contamination has also resulted from fires and explosions. One such event on the Swanson River Field resulted in an eight-year, $40-million effort to remove PCBs from refuge soils. Many of these problems went unnoticed for years, and it is possible others are still unknown.

USFWS has also been responsible for some of the contamination of Kenai NWR. In the past, when understanding of risks posed by such substances was in its

infancy, herbicides, including Agent Orange, were used on a limited basis on the refuge. As experimental alternatives to controlled burns, chemicals were used to determine if they could effectively kill spruce and taller deciduous trees to encourage growth of species preferred as moose browse. Other potentially toxic chemicals were used to treat fence posts against rotting. The last documented use of such materials was in 1966; no herbicides or pesticides are in use on the refuge today.

Other potential sources of contamination include Formerly Used Defense sites (FUDs), mining operations, development near refuge boundaries, and recreational analysts had not determined if there might be a reasonable alternative to cutting a road through the designated Wilderness, an alternative that would also address the health and safety concerns of King Cove residents. Such a road would, after all, irreversibly alter the wilderness character of the refuge, and have serious impacts on waterfowl and wetlands of international significance.

The standoff continued until the 11th hour, when Alaska Sen. Ted Stevens and Pres. Bill Clinton's chief of staff, Erskine Bowles, reached a compromise. Instead of funding the road, which some estimated would have cost as much as $30 million, section 353 of the 1999 Omnibus and Emergency Supplemental Appropriations Act included $20 million to be used to build a road on King Cove Corp. lands providing access to a new dock and marine facilities, including a hovercraft or ferry to provide more dependable transportation between the two communities; $2.5 million to build a new 9,600-square-foot King Cove health clinic, including dental services, an expanded emergency room, and telemedicine equipment allowing direct consultation with, and digital transfer of X-rays to physicians at Anchorage's Alaska Native Health Center; and $15 million for improvements to the King Cove Air Strip. This compromise, in Senator Stevens's words, "provides for the health and safety of the Alaska Native people of King Cove and still protects the refuge."

Currently, the funds for the proposed hovercraft facility and the road associated with it have been transferred to the Aleutians East Borough. The U.S. Army Corps of Engineers has circulated a Draft Environmental Impact Statement (DEIS) evaluating the proposed hovercraft project and alternatives for providing an improved transportation link to it. A final decision identifying and authorizing the selected alternative should be issued by the Corps in summer 2003.

The $2.5 million for the clinic, augmented by an additional $1.6 million from the Denali Commission (created by federal law in 1998 to address the infrastructure needs of rural Alaska), was transferred to the Borough as well, and the new health center opened its doors in early 2002.

Following negotiations with USFWS on the transfer of the $15 million appropriated for improvements to the King Cove Air Strip, the Alaska Department of Transportation and Public Facilities eventually declined to sign the draft grant agreement, having concluded that conversion of the current King Cove Air Strip is neither prudent nor feasible.

It's expected the compromise transportation alternative, consisting of the hovercraft facility and access to it, as

Mountainous terrain characterizes the area north of King Cove and east of Lenard Harbor. Any road built between King Cove and Cold Bay would cross varied types of habitat. (Courtesy USFWS)

authorized by Congress, will be completed in the near future, achieving the goal of improving health care and safety of King Cove residents while protecting Izembek Wilderness.

Arctic NWR: Oil Drilling on the Coastal Plain?

If there is a single issue facing Alaska's national wildlife refuges that the American public is likely to be aware of, this is the one. For more than 20 years the question of whether to allow oil and gas exploration and development on the Arctic NWR's coastal plain has been one

of the most hotly debated conservation issues in the United States.

No one knows how much economically recoverable oil might be found under the approximately 1.5-million-acre coastal plain. The best informed estimate, appearing in USGS's 2001 fact sheet on the issue, predicts a mean value of 5.2 billion barrels of economically recoverable oil when prices for North Slope crude oil are at $24 per barrel, based upon 1996 dollars. Proponents of development say tapping this supply would reduce the country's dependence on foreign oil, enhance national security, and shore up Alaska's economy. Opponents point out the 1002 area represents only five percent of Alaska's arctic coastal plain, and is the only portion of it specifically closed to oil and gas development. They maintain the risk to various species, such as the Porcupine caribou herd and polar bears, as well as the irreversible damage to the area's wilderness character, are too great a price for the potential rewards.

So contentious is the argument over oil development on Arctic NWR's coastal

LEFT, TOP: *Gravel roads have been success-fully built in the Prudhoe Bay region, whose terrain resembles that of Arctic NWR's coastal plain. Snow and ice roads are used during winter. (Courtesy USFWS)*

LEFT: *55-gallon oil drums lie abandoned in an unidentified area of North Slope tundra. Environmental damage from oil and gas development concerns many opposed to drilling in Arctic NWR. (Courtesy USFWS)*

plain that advocates on both sides of the issue sometimes allow themselves to be swayed by emotion rather than fact. It has become, in some quarters, a war over symbols rather than science.

Looking Ahead: Quality of Experience vs. Unlimited Access

The examples presented above have generated widespread media attention, but the largest looming challenge to Alaska's refuges is far less dramatic. Newsworthy or not, however, it concerns the nature of USFWS's stewardship of the public lands in its trust. Put simply, the question is this: How can land managers protect the quality of experience visitors to Alaska's refuges expect and deserve while continuing to provide access? More specifically, how can USFWS manage the increase in public use of refuges now to avoid having to decrease public use after it has reached unacceptable levels?

Most of the national wildlife refuges in Alaska are remote and relatively difficult to access. That remoteness creates a certain expectation in the minds of those who visit. They want to see wilderness. They would prefer to not encounter any other visitors during their adventure. They want to savor the feeling of setting foot upon truly wild country. They do not want to find trash when they pull their raft to the bank to camp for the night.

The problem has even surfaced on Togiak NWR, far from the road system. The Goodnews, Togiak, and Kanektok Rivers are important to subsistence users and to commercially guided and unguided

recreational river floaters and anglers. The growing popularity of these rivers has caused concern about pollution and overcrowding. Refuge managers are considering several courses of action: restricting the number of floaters allowed on a river per day; setting up a registration system for noncommercial users to better assess the impact this group may be having; or, as is widely done now in the Lower 48, requiring visitors to pack human waste out in special containers.

Togiak is still in the early stages of studying the situation, but concerns there should serve as a statewide wake-up call. The challenge of balancing public use and public satisfaction needs to be faced by refuge managers across Alaska. It requires a difficult balancing act, and might force managers to make unpopular

Off-road-vehicle tracks can remain in soft arctic ground. Permafrost underlies the entire North Slope and partial melting of upper layers occurs each brief summer. (Tom Walker)

decisions. Taking no action, however, could result in many of Alaska's national wildlife refuges being loved to death. ∎

Refuge People Today

Lee Anne Ayres, Flying Biologist

Some people spend years fantasizing about moving to Alaska, only to be driven south by cold and darkness before their first long winter ends. But Selawik NWR wildlife biologist/pilot Lee Anne Ayres's career turns that cliche on its ear.

"Coming to Alaska wasn't a dream of mine or anything," she says. "In fact, before I came to Kotzebue to work on my Master's thesis on Dall sheep, I couldn't have found it on a map. That was in 1983. It's a surprise to me that I've stayed so long, but this area has been a wonderful fit. I just love my work, and can't imagine

finding a job in the Lower 48 that would allow me to do what I do here."

Ayres's first position after completing her graduate thesis at the University of California Berkeley was with the National Park Service. After receiving her degree, she became that agency's first permanent wildlife biologist in northwestern Alaska. She worked for the National Park Service through 1990, then took a position with the State of Alaska as the assistant area biologist in Kotzebue, a job that enabled her to focus more on wildlife and wildlife management issues. Then in 1999, USFWS hired Ayres as a wildlife biologist/ pilot on Selawik NWR. She'd been a

LEFT: *Lee Anne Ayres, pilot and biologist for Selawik NWR, stops at the Selawik refuge cabin slough during spring 2001. Alaska has been her home since 1983. (John Bertrand, courtesy Lee Anne Ayres)*

FACING PAGE: *Tufted puffins perch on a rocky cliff in the Pribilofs. This species nests in burrows dug into the soil or in rock crevices. Wildlife research is an essential aspect of Alaska's national wildlife refuge staff. (Tom Bol Photography)*

recreational pilot for 10 years, owned her own plane, and had done some flying for the state. The opportunity to more fully integrate flying into her job interested her. She was also eager to work with Leslie Kerr, who was refuge manager then, and excited at the chance to continue working with moose and caribou while also being involved with other resources and species. The refuge system's mandate encourages a focus on the different components of ecosystems and how they interact.

Ayres says, "Typically people in public service tend to stay with one agency and move up the career ladder, which often requires moving locations. By changing agencies every eight or nine years I may have sacrificed some job seniority, but I've built up local seniority in northwest Alaska. I really enjoy the people and country here. It takes time to learn about the area's unique resources and simply how to get around in this country ... so I believe the years I've spent here have made me progressively better at doing my job. There has also been some career continuity. When I was with Park Service and the State, I had opportunities to work with the Selawik NWR staff on cooperative projects, so I was fairly familiar with the Fish and Wildlife Service, and especially the Selawik refuge, long before taking my current position. As a result I've settled right in here."

One of the byproducts of Ayres's local seniority is an acquired understanding of, and sensitivity to, local issues. This becomes apparent when she discusses an ongoing whitefish study she ranks among the most rewarding projects she's currently involved in.

Common throughout most of Alaska except during winter, Pacific loons breed on tundra lakes or in coniferous forests. (Robin Brandt)

"It was obvious that we didn't know very much about whitefish or local fishing practices for these species, and that we needed to learn more. These fish are among the main sources of protein for local people, so it's important to consider that reliance, and to incorporate the knowledge that people of this region have accumulated about whitefish into any management practices we might undertake. In general, this can be difficult to do. I think we often do a good job of documenting local knowledge, but aren't always as successful at integrating it into our work, perhaps because it is a different type of information than we're used to dealing with.

"The whitefish studies provided a perfect opportunity to explore this approach, because the local people here know so much more about this resource than we do. Leslie Kerr helped initiate this process, and current refuge manager Gene Peltola has continued to support it. We work closely with Susan Georgette, who covers subsistence issues in Kotzebue for the State of Alaska, to collect local information on Selawik whitefish. The idea was to find out what people in the region know already, and use that as a springboard to direct further research.

"We've come up with some fascinating results. The residents of Selawik have been wonderfully cooperative in providing information and granting interviews. Many of them have detailed knowledge of whitefish ecology. They know, for example, where the fish overwinter, because they go to these places in the spring to fish. They don't, however, know much about where the fish spawn, because they don't traditionally fish during that time of the year. This is where research can fill in the blanks, and provide a piece of knowledge essential to both biologists and to subsistence users. By identifying this essential habitat we can work together, on and off the refuge, to ensure the future health of these populations. Many of the people we interviewed were also interested in obtaining help from fisheries scientists in identifying the various species of whitefish in the area. There are local names for them, but people are unsure whether these actually represent different species, or just fish from different tributaries that are slightly different in taste or appearance. This will also be another area we'll try to focus on as the project goes forward."

In Ayres's work on this study and others on a land unit that, though small for Alaska refuges, still covers more than two million acres, transportation typically means taking to the air. She is a self-described conservative pilot. "I look for the biggest lake, the biggest gravel bar and the best conditions. I don't like to scare myself," she says. Ayres clearly loves flying, both on the job and recreationally. When asked if there was a single refuge experience that stands out in her memory, she named two. Both incidents feature aircraft, and it's significant that she admits to struggling with the contradiction they expose.

"I remember landing at our refuge cabin in the spring after tracking moose," she recalls. "I was out by myself and needed to refuel, so I landed on skis on the lagoon in front of the cabin. It was a spectacular early-spring day. The birds were beginning to come back, and every patch of ground where the snow had melted off was alive. You have to understand how quiet it becomes up here in the winter, after the migratory species leave. The whole experience of spending the day flying over the country, then landing at this remote place and hearing cranes and geese calling, and feeling that first warmth in the sun again after a long winter, was just delightful. I sat there and listened and soaked in the sights and the sounds and the sun and thought to myself, 'I have a wonderful job.'

"The other memory involves a plane, too. This was in July, and I'd landed on a lake to take a break. I just needed to sit down and not be moving for a while. We were preparing to do white-fronted geese surveys, and there was a group of white-fronts on the lake, along with some loons and scoters. When I landed they flushed to the water's edge, but since they were molting they stayed on the lake and I sat out on the plane's float and watched them. They kept an eye on the plane, but soon settled back to what they were doing.

"After a few moments, however, the birds became really agitated and nervous. It was quite awhile later I finally heard the plane that was causing all the commotion. I was impressed at how far away it had been when the birds first reacted to it, and at how great an effect it had. It reminded me that, even when we're doing things for the resource, things that need to be done, we have to be aware of the impacts we're having on what we're trying to protect. That moment wasn't as rosy and wonderful as hearing spring arrive around the refuge cabin, but it taught me something that I've tried to remember. We don't have the same senses as other creatures, and we can never assume that what we do will have the same impact upon them that it might upon us."

Teaching people about wildlife, from mice to muskox, is one of the tasks of refuge information technicians. Muskox thrive on Nunivak Island. The animals' underwool is spun into thread used to knit warm, lightweight garments. (Steven Kazlowski)

Orville Lind and the Role of Refuge Information Technicians

As anyone who has had to explain his or her work to the general public knows, communicating, even when language and culture are shared, can be a challenge. It is also essential. Without the understanding and support of an informed public, all the good science in the world will not enable the national wildlife refuge system to protect resources in its charge. But even in the most homogeneous societies, politics, preconceptions, and personalities contrive to close the ears and the minds of many people refuge staff most need to reach.

Imagine, then, the difficulties of taking those same messages to stakeholders whose livelihood is impacted by decisions made. Imagine, too, that these men and women share a culture that is decidedly different from that of most USFWS personnel, and that for many of them English is a second language.

This was the situation USFWS faced in the early 1980s in parts of rural Alaska. Distrust was widespread, and some villages refused to contribute information to USFWS waterfowl surveys or to participate in village or tribal council meetings. Some wouldn't even allow USFWS personnel to give school presentations in their communities.

In 1984, a new program was initiated on the Yukon Delta NWR to address these problems. Hiring village residents under the local hire provisions of ANILCA, the Refuge Information Technician (RIT) Program was designed to collect local harvest data and share information about declining goose populations with Alaska villages. It was the first of its kind to be organized by USFWS in Alaska, and is successful today, with RITs on duty in Togiak, Alaska Peninsula, Becharof, Yukon Delta, Selawik, Innoko, Tetlin, and Arctic NWRs.

In the beginning, however, USFWS's new RITs found their jobs were not necessarily easy. Alaska Peninsula and Becharof NWRs ranger Orville Lind, who started his career with USFWS through the RIT program in 1991 and has since trained new RITs for Selawik and Alaska Peninsula NWRs, remembers, "When I was hired, most of the villagers I'd talk to didn't even know what the Fish and Wildlife Service was. To most of them, a person in uniform was either a state trooper or with the Alaska Department of Fish and Game. And many of these people considered Fish and Game to be bad guys. They took away guns, and food, and sometimes family members accused of breaking the law while pursuing their subsistence lifestyles.

Orville Lind's job as a refuge information technician includes giving presentations and working closely with local residents on issues such as subsistence. (Courtesy USFWS)

Rising from the ocean are 5,315-foot Mount Carlisle, in the background, a volcano last active in 1987 and 5,676-foot Mount Cleveland, which erupted most recently in February and March 2001, sending an ash plume 30,000 feet above sea level on March 19. Active volcanoes sometimes hamper scientific work in the Aleutians. (Scott Darsney)

"So if I went to someone's door in my uniform and said, 'Hi, I'm Orville with the Fish and Wildlife Service. I've come to check out how many birds you've harvested this season,' I'd find myself staring at a closed door. I wouldn't get very far.

"Our job was difficult. We were trying to gather information, but whenever one of us would show up the locals would suddenly become very quiet. The attitude was, 'I'm not going to tell this fool anything.' The distrust was so great that sometimes even our relatives would not go hunting with us. This hurt, because in our tradition, families always gather food together. Many people in the villages looked at the RITs as outsiders. They feared that they would get in trouble for whatever they might tell us. So in the early days we were able to gather little information, and much of what we got was probably incorrect.

"The first challenge of the RITs was to build trust. This was done by visiting each home in the village. These visits had to be social, not right to the point with questions. Once we were invited into a home, we knew we had to spend time — not 'government time' but 'village time' —

time talking with the family and sharing with them what we, and the mission of the Service, are about. We took that time, village time, to help the people understand why we need to do surveys, and how our biologists can use this information to make wise conservation decisions so that locals and their children can continue their subsistence lifestyles, and so others can continue to enjoy Alaska's resources.

"Language was another complicating factor. We RITs could speak to the people in the villages in their own language. I, for example, am of Aleut descent and speak the Alutiiq language, but translating

government-speak into terms that made sense to the people was sometimes difficult. As we all know, if you don't understand something it doesn't stay with you.

" … There were other linguistic difficulties. The harvest forms that we used labeled the birds in English. Worse yet, the illustrations on the bird survey forms weren't in color, and this made some people nervous. What if they picked the wrong bird based on the confusing black and white illustrations? Could they be sent to jail? The RITs could identify each bird in the local language, but even that

ABOVE: *Vernon Byrd takes notes on Chagulak Island, one of the central Aleutians' Islands of Four Mountains. Foxes, introduced on many Aleutian Islands in the early 1900s, were never deposited on Chagulak, and bird life fared better here. (Courtesy Vernon Byrd)*

ABOVE, RIGHT: *Vernon Byrd played an instrumental role in the population recovery of the Aleutian Canada goose. (Courtesy USFWS)*

wasn't foolproof. In another village a hundred miles away the same bird's name might be pronounced differently.

"Slowly though, through patience, and through careful communication, trust began to grow. We knew we were successful at getting our information across if people offered us tea and something to eat. It became a joke that you could tell the most successful RITs by watching their waistlines.

"As time went on, the roles of the RITs grew. We began to bring programs into schools to increase awareness of species that are in trouble, we worked to build and maintain trusting working relation-ships with other agencies, councils, and corporations. We helped villagers understand that the Service's mission and concerns for wildlife are right in line with the teachings of our elders.

"And in the years since 1984 the RIT program has made a difference. We can see it in population increases in some of our goose species, we can see it in the simple fact that most locals now welcome us into their homes and schools, and rely on us to keep them informed and updated about current wildlife issues.

"There is, of course, work to be done. There are still many threats to our wildlife resources. But we know that, whatever challenges the future might bring, as long as we stay focused, and remember to stay on village time, the RIT program will be successful, and we will be doing our part to make sure that our children, and their children, will inherit an Alaska as rich, or richer, in resources and tradition than the one our Elders handed down to us."

Vernon Byrd, Your Man in the Aleutians

Tiny Buldir Island, only four miles long by almost two miles wide and about 300 miles from Siberia, is the most isolated of the Aleutian chain. It is a lump of grass-covered soil and rock surrounded by deep water and whipped by almost continual winds. Biologist Vernon Byrd remembers his initial arrival on Buldir as the most wonderful moment of his more than 30 years with USFWS in Alaska.

"I'd heard so much about, thought so much about the island, and the Aleutian Canada geese, that actually stepping ashore on Buldir for the first time was unbelievable," Byrd says. "I'd been eager to see it for quite a while, probably because it's the most isolated island in the chain, the most pristine. I'd worked in the Aleutians when I was in the navy, I'd been on Adak and Shemya, and the Aleutians seemed like paradise to me. But I knew Buldir would be the best of the best, it was my Aleutian Mecca. When I landed there in 1972 I thought I'd died and gone to heaven."

Byrd, a North Carolinian by birth, first came to Alaska in 1968 with the navy and was stationed on Adak Island. That early Aleutian experience shaped much of his career with USFWS. His first position, in 1971, took him to Cold Bay, where he served as a biological technician at Izembek NWR. The following spring, however, Byrd was assigned to set up USFWS's first office in the Aleutians. That job took him home to Adak, where he became manager of the Aleutian Islands NWR, now part of Alaska Maritime NWR.

The early 1970s was an historic period for USFWS in the Aleutians, and the new refuge manager was quickly caught up, along with Bob "Sea Otter" Jones, whom Byrd notes was "sort of my hero," in the monumental task of trying to bring the endangered Aleutian Canada goose back from presumed extinction. While Byrd recognizes the key part he played in recovery of this species is a huge accomplishment, he thinks it pointed out an even bigger job yet to be done.

"Removing nonnative foxes to allow the recovery of the Aleutian Canada goose was the first time we faced up to the problem of invasive species on the islands, but we quickly saw that our job wouldn't be over once the geese were recovered. The only truly final objective is the recovery of the natural diversity of the refuge. So we've continued that work and expanded the program to try to restore the diversity of the islands through management of a number of invasive species, including foxes, rats, and ground squirrels. Clearly the goose was the impetus for this ongoing effort, which remains as one of the major challenges we face on the refuge to this day."

As important as they have been, recovery of the Aleutian Canada goose and related work to control invasive species on the refuge have been reactive in nature, driven by problems that were already apparent. Perhaps as significant is proactive work being done, particularly ecological monitoring of the Aleutian chain. Byrd explains: "Our refuge is so far-flung that it provides a unique opportunity to monitor top level predators in several Alaska marine ecosystems. Essentially we're attempting to study seabirds as indicators of change in the marine system. To do this we're working with a network of partners, including the National Marine Fisheries Service, the State of Alaska, and nongovernmental organizations and universities, essentially trying to tease out threads of information about ecosystem processes. We're using this broad network of different knowledge bases to collect and collate information and post it on the Internet in an annual summary that is already being used to test hypotheses about ecosystem change.

" ... We're in the process of defining normal change, which will then help us better recognize abnormal change and determine what might be causing it. ... this research could ... help us learn how to more effectively direct management actions when we're faced with a real problem, such as an oil spill or another sort of pollution event, but probably as

Northern fur seals bask in the sun in the Pribilof Islands, where fur traders found the species in the mid 1700s. (Loren Taft)

important, if less obvious, it can help us avoid wasting time and resources whipsawing in every direction in response to a completely natural change, a cyclic drop in a species population, for example."

It's clear from Byrd's enthusiasm for his work that his years with the refuge system haven't taken any shine off of his dedication to wildlife conservation. He remains a passionate proponent of

Hunting and fishing have always been part of Mike Rearden's life, so wildlife management comes naturally to him. His father, Jim Rearden, was also a wildlife manager. (Courtesy USFWS)

refuges, and a visionary when it comes to describing their value today and imagining what they can be.

"The national wildlife refuge system is the only network of lands in the world to be set aside specifically for wildlife. Certainly the Park Service and Forest Service properties include some important habitat, but refuges are the only lands with a mandate to consider the needs of wildlife first. Nationally and internationally, these lands do some of the heaviest lifting in conservation work today. And our refuges can carry those heavy loads, in the form, for example, of habitat restoration and endangered species recovery, because we do have that singular mandate."

Mike Rearden: A Lifetime of Experience

Lifelong Alaskan Mike Rearden began his career with USFWS in 1975, working in public affairs in the regional office in Anchorage. In less than a year, however, he had moved to Kodiak NWR. Alaska's refuges have shaped the rest of his career. Given the man's background, this isn't surprising. When asked what prompted him to leave the regional office after less than a year, his answer is straightforward: "It was working in the regional office that convinced me to head for a refuge! I didn't enjoy living in Anchorage. I needed to be in a more rural location."

Rearden was born in Fairbanks but grew up in Homer. His early years kept him involved in and helped him develop an appreciation for the wild world around him.

"As a young kid on the Kenai in the '50s and '60s," Rearden says, "I was always hunting or fishing it seems. We depended on moose as our main source of red meat, so the annual moose hunt was a big thing. We also hunted waterfowl, and did a lot of both sport and subsistence fishing." It was the kind of outdoor-centered childhood that has molded many a biologist, but the young Rearden also had the benefit of a more powerful inspiration.

"My father, Jim Rearden, has had the greatest influence on my career. He was a wildlife manager himself. Dad came to Alaska in 1947 as a temporary [USFWS] employee, and went on to establish the wildlife studies department at the University of Alaska Fairbanks in the fall of 1950. ... So even before I left Homer to attend [UAF], I was used to dinner table conversations about things like the biological carrying capacity of a piece of land or water."

After graduating from UAF and enduring his brief stint in Anchorage, Rearden served as Kodiak NWR's Native liaison for four years. He also started flying for USFWS as a refuge pilot while on the Emerald Isle.

"The weather down there is tough, it's windy and foggy," he remembers. "It was kind of a difficult place for a beginning pilot to learn his stuff. You might say I gained a lot of experience in a really short time down there, and some of it was very memorable. But I also had the opportunity to do bear surveys and eagle surveys, and to work around Karluk Lake, which I still think is one of the prettiest places in Alaska."

Rearden left Kodiak for Yukon Delta NWR in 1980. Except for a four-year interruption during which he served in Kotzebue as the refuge manager for Selawik NWR, the Yukon-Kuskokwim Delta has been his home for the last 20-plus years, first during a stint as assistant refuge manager/pilot and then, after returning to Yukon Delta in 1995, as refuge manager. "The most important thing we're doing," says Rearden, "is working with the more than 40 villages within our refuge's boundaries. The people in these villages are our neighbors. The villages own land within our borders, and their residents also use refuge lands for subsistence activities. So communication and cooperation with these partners is probably our most important job.

"It can be our greatest challenge, as well. We have many villages to deal with, and the issue of subsistence is vital to the

Banding Canada geese helps Mike Rearden and other biologists determine migration patterns. (Courtesy USFWS)

people in all of them. Everyone has a keen interest in what we're doing, and most want to be involved in the development of any regulations or restrictions that might affect their livelihood.

"There are many facets to this, but I'm probably proudest of what we've accomplished in the few years that we've been directly involved with managing subsistence fisheries on refuge lands. It's been a huge challenge, but working with the state and with local people on the responsible management of refuge fishery resources has been incredibly rewarding. Because these issues are so crucial, especially in light of the weak salmon runs on both the Yukon and Kuskokwim Rivers the last few years, good communication among our partners has been absolutely essential. We've tried to stay in front of the issues, working with local newspapers and radio stations, conducting countless village meetings, to keep people aware of what we might have to do before the fact, and make sure they understand why a particular restriction is essential to the future of the resource. We've found that, when we do that job well enough, people might not like what we do ... but they'll understand and comply with the regulations.

"My wife, Nita (Prince) Rearden, has been an invaluable helpmate as I've worked on these issues, as she has in my career in general. Nita is Yup'ik, and a teacher with more than 20 years

experience. She's taught me most of what I understand about local issues and about Yup'ik culture. We've also raised four children together.

"... I hope my sons and daughter will inherit a healthy national wildlife refuge system to pass along to their children. From my personal perspective, the refuge system is a way of guaranteeing that future generations of Alaskans and of people from around the globe will still have wild lands and wildlife available to them. As a hunter and fisherman, as a person who has used these resources all my life, I think it's especially important that our refuges allow these uses, and do so in a manner that assures they will be able to continue to allow them for generations to come. I believe there's adequate room on our refuges for sport uses and nonconsumptive uses and

Mike Rearden pilots his floatplane in Innoko NWR. He is currently refuge manager of Yukon Delta NWR. (Tom Walker)

subsistence uses if we manage our habitat and wildlife properly.

"And I can renew that belief every spring, by simply going out to the coastal areas of the refuge when the migratory birds return to what is one of the most important nesting areas in North America. To be out there and see the waterfowl, passerines, and shorebirds arriving from all across the country and even from other continents, to hear the squawking and talking, to smell the smells and generally drink in the atmosphere of it all is to wonder at the wild world's productivity and capacity for regeneration. It always boosts my morale, and reminds me, if I need reminding, why wild lands, and national wildlife refuges, are so important." ■

Bibliography

Henning, Robert A., ed. *Up the Koyukuk*. Vol. 10, No. 4 *ALASKA GEOGRAPHIC®*. Anchorage: Alaska Geographic Society, 1983.

Hunter, Celia and Ginny Wood. *Alaska National Interest Lands*. Vol. 8, No. 4 *ALASKA GEOGRAPHIC®*. Edited by Robert A. Henning, Barbara Olds, and Penny Rennick. Anchorage: Alaska Geographic Society, 1981.

Rennick, Penny, ed. *Arctic National Wildlife Refuge*. Vol. 20, No. 3 *ALASKA GEOGRAPHIC®*. Anchorage: Alaska Geographic Society, 1993.

—. *Moose, Caribou and Muskox*. Vol. 23, No. 4 *ALASKA GEOGRAPHIC®*. Anchorage: Alaska Geographic Society, 1997.

—. *The Lower Yukon River*. Vol. 17, No. 4 *ALASKA GEOGRAPHIC®*. Anchorage: Alaska Geographic Society, 1991.

Richardson, Tim and Dave Cline, eds. *Kodiak Bears and the* Exxon Valdez: *A Conservation Saga in Alaska's Kodiak Archipelago*. Kodiak, Alaska: Kodiak Brown Bear Trust, 2000.

Websites

http://alaskamaritime.fws.gov
http://alaskapeninsula.fws.gov
http://arctic.fws.gov
http://becharof.fws.gov
http://innoko.fws.gov
http://izembek.fws.gov
http://kanuti.fws.gov
http://kenai.fws.gov
http://kodiak.fws.gov
http://koyukuk.fws.gov
http://nowitna.fws.gov
http://selawik.fws.gov
http://tetlin.fws.gov
http://togiak.fws.gov
http://yukondelta.fws.gov
http://yukonflats.fws.gov
http://www.r7.fws.gov/ (USFWS Alaska Region)

Refuge Headquarters and Visitor Centers

(Address correspondence to Refuge Manager)

Alaska Maritime NWR
2355 Kachemak Bay Dr., Ste. 101
Homer, AK 99603
Phone: (907) 235-6546

Alaska Peninsula/Becharof NWRs
King Salmon Inter-Agency Visitor Center
PO Box 298, King Salmon, AK 99613
Phone: (907) 246-4250

Arctic NWR
101 - 12th Avenue, Room 236, Box 20
Fairbanks, AK 99701
Phone: (907) 456-0250

Innoko NWR
PO Box 69, McGrath, AK 99627
Phone: (907) 524-3251

Izembek NWR
PO Box 127, Cold Bay, AK 99571
Phone: (907) 532-2445

Kanuti NWR
101 - 12th Avenue, Box 11
Fairbanks, AK 99701
Phone: (907) 456-0329

Kenai NWR
PO Box 2139, Soldotna, AK 99669
Phone: (907) 262-7021

Kodiak NWR
1390 Buskin River Rd., Kodiak, AK 99615
Phone: (907) 487-2600

Koyukuk/Northern Innoko and Nowitna NWRs
PO Box 287, Galena, AK 99741
Phone: (907) 656-1231

Selawik NWR
PO Box 270, Kotzebue, AK 99752
Phone: (907) 442-3799

Tetlin NWR
PO Box 779, Tok, AK 99780
Phone: (907) 883-5312

Togiak NWR
PO Box 270, Dillingham, AK 99576
Phone: (907) 842-1063

Yukon Delta NWR
PO Box 346, Bethel, AK 99559
Phone: (907) 543-3151

Yukon Flats NWR
101 - 12th Avenue, Room 264
Fairbanks, AK 99701
Phone: (907) 456-0440 ■

Index

■

ALASKA GEOGRAPHIC. Back Issues

Membership in The Alaska Geographic Society includes a subscription to *ALASKA GEOGRAPHIC*®, the Society's colorful, award-winning quarterly. Contact us for current membership rates or to request a copy of our free catalog.

The *ALASKA GEOGRAPHIC*® back issues listed below can be ordered directly from us. **NOTE:** This list was current in early 2003. If more than a year has elapsed since that time, be sure to contact us before ordering to check prices and availability of back issues, particularly those marked "Limited."

When ordering back issues please add $5 for the first book and $2 for each additional book ordered to cover shipping and handling. Inquire for shipping rates to non-U.S. addresses. To order, send check or money order (U.S. funds) or VISA or MasterCard information (including expiration date and daytime phone number) with list of titles desired to:

ALASKA GEOGRAPHIC.

P.O. Box 93370 • Anchorage, AK 99509-3370
Phone (907) 562-0164 • Toll free (888) 255-6697
Fax (907) 562-0479 • e-mail: info@akgeo.com

The North Slope, Vol. 1, No. 1. Out of print.
One Man's Wilderness, Vol. 1, No. 2. Out of print.
Admiralty...Island in Contention, Vol. 1, No. 3. $9.95.
Fisheries of the North Pacific, Vol. 1, No. 4. Out of print.
Alaska-Yukon Wild Flowers, Vol. 2, No. 1. Out of print.
Richard Harrington's Yukon, Vol. 2, No. 2. Out of print.
Prince William Sound, Vol. 2, No. 3. Out of print.
Yakutat: The Turbulent Crescent, Vol. 2, No. 4. Out of print.
Glacier Bay: Old Ice, New Land, Vol. 3, No. 1. Out of print.
The Land: Eye of the Storm, Vol. 3, No. 2. Out of print.
Richard Harrington's Antarctic, Vol. 3, No. 3. $9.95.
The Silver Years, Vol. 3, No. 4. $24.95. Limited.
Alaska's Volcanoes, Vol. 4, No. 1. Out of print.
The Brooks Range, Vol. 4, No. 2. Out of print.
Kodiak: Island of Change, Vol. 4, No. 3. Out of print.
Wilderness Proposals, Vol. 4, No. 4. Out of print.
Cook Inlet Country, Vol. 5, No. 1. Out of print.
Southeast: Alaska's Panhandle, Vol. 5, No. 2. Out of print.
Bristol Bay Basin, Vol. 5, No. 3. Out of print.
Alaska Whales and Whaling, Vol. 5, No. 4. $19.95.
Yukon-Kuskokwim Delta, Vol. 6, No. 1. Out of print.
Aurora Borealis, Vol. 6, No. 2. $24.95. Limited
Alaska's Native People, Vol. 6, No. 3. $29.95. Limited.
The Stikine River, Vol. 6, No. 4. $9.95.
Alaska's Great Interior, Vol. 7, No. 1. $19.95.
Photographic Geography of Alaska, Vol. 7, No. 2. Out of print.
The Aleutians, Vol. 7, No. 3. Out of print.

Klondike Lost, Vol. 7, No. 4. Out of print.
Wrangell-Saint Elias, Vol. 8, No. 1. Out of print.
Alaska Mammals, Vol. 8, No. 2. Out of print.
The Kotzebue Basin, Vol. 8, No. 3. Out of print.
Alaska National Interest Lands, Vol. 8, No. 4. $19.95.
*Alaska's Glaciers, Vol. 9, No. 1. Rev. 1993. $24.95. Limited.
Sitka and Its Ocean/Island World, Vol. 9, No. 2. Out of print.
Islands of the Seals: The Pribilofs, Vol. 9, No. 3. $9.95.
Alaska's Oil/Gas & Minerals Industry, Vol. 9, No. 4. $9.95.
Adventure Roads North, Vol. 10, No. 1. $9.95.
Anchorage and the Cook Inlet Basin, Vol. 10, No. 2. $19.95.
Alaska's Salmon Fisheries, Vol. 10, No. 3. $9.95.
Up the Koyukuk, Vol. 10, No. 4. $9.95.
Nome, Vol. 11, No. 1. Out of print.
Alaska's Farms and Gardens, Vol. 11, No. 2. $19.95.
Chilkat River Valley, Vol. 11, No. 3. $9.95.
Alaska Steam, Vol. 11, No. 4. $19.95.
Northwest Territories, Vol. 12, No. 1. $9.95.
Alaska's Forest Resources, Vol. 12, No. 2. $9.95.
Alaska Native Arts and Crafts, Vol. 12, No. 3. $24.95.
Our Arctic Year, Vol. 12, No. 4. $19.95.
* Where Mountains Meet the Sea, Vol. 13, No. 1. $19.95.
Backcountry Alaska, Vol. 13, No. 2. $9.95.
British Columbia's Coast, Vol. 13, No. 3. $9.95.
Lake Clark/Lake Iliamna, Vol. 13, No. 4. Out of print.
Dogs of the North, Vol. 14, No. 1. Out of print.
South/Southeast Alaska, Vol. 14, No. 2. $24.95. Limited.
Alaska's Seward Peninsula, Vol. 14, No. 3. $19.95.
The Upper Yukon Basin, Vol. 14, No. 4. $19.95.
Glacier Bay: Icy Wilderness, Vol. 15, No. 1. Out of print.
Dawson City, Vol. 15, No. 2. $19.95.
Denali, Vol. 15, No. 3. $9.95.
The Kuskokwim River, Vol. 15, No. 4. $19.95.
Katmai Country, Vol. 16, No. 1. $19.95.
North Slope Now, Vol. 16, No. 2. $9.95.
The Tanana Basin, Vol. 16, No. 3. $9.95.
* The Copper Trail, Vol. 16, No. 4. $19.95.
* The Nushagak Basin, Vol. 17, No. 1. $19.95.
* Juneau, Vol. 17, No. 2. Out of print.
* The Middle Yukon River, Vol. 17, No. 3. $19.95.
* The Lower Yukon River, Vol. 17, No. 4. $19.95.
* Alaska's Weather, Vol. 18, No. 1. $9.95.
* Alaska's Volcanoes, Vol. 18, No. 2. $24.95. Limited
Admiralty Island: Fortress of Bears, Vol. 18, No. 3. Out of print.
Unalaska/Dutch Harbor, Vol. 18, No. 4. Out of print.
* Skagway: A Legacy of Gold, Vol. 19, No. 1. $9.95.
Alaska: The Great Land, Vol. 19, No. 2. $9.95.
Kodiak, Vol. 19, No. 3. Out of print.
Alaska's Railroads, Vol. 19, No. 4. $19.95.
Prince William Sound, Vol. 20, No. 1. $9.95.
Southeast Alaska, Vol. 20, No. 2. $19.95.
Arctic National Wildlife Refuge, Vol. 20, No. 3. $19.95.
Alaska's Bears, Vol. 20, No. 4. $19.95.

The Alaska Peninsula, Vol. 21, No. 1. $19.95.
The Kenai Peninsula, Vol. 21, No. 2. $19.95.
People of Alaska, Vol. 21, No. 3. $19.95.
Prehistoric Alaska, Vol. 21, No. 4. $19.95.
Fairbanks, Vol. 22, No. 1. $19.95.
The Aleutian Islands, Vol. 22, No. 2. $19.95.
Rich Earth: Alaska's Mineral Industry, Vol. 22, No. 3. $19.95.
World War II in Alaska, Vol. 22, No. 4. $24.95. Limited.
Anchorage, Vol. 23, No. 1. $21.95.
Native Cultures in Alaska, Vol. 23, No. 2. $19.95.
The Brooks Range, Vol. 23, No. 3. $19.95.
Moose, Caribou and Muskox, Vol. 23, No. 4. $19.95.
Alaska's Southern Panhandle, Vol. 24, No. 1. $19.95.
The Golden Gamble, Vol. 24, No. 2. $19.95.
Commercial Fishing in Alaska, Vol. 24, No. 3. $19.95.
Alaska's Magnificent Eagles, Vol. 24, No. 4. $19.95.
Steve McCutcheon's Alaska, Vol. 25, No. 1. $21.95.
Yukon Territory, Vol. 25, No. 2. $21.95.
Climbing Alaska, Vol. 25, No. 3. $21.95.
Frontier Flight, Vol. 25, No. 4. $21.95.
Restoring Alaska: Legacy of an Oil Spill, Vol. 26, No. 1. $21.95.
World Heritage Wilderness, Vol. 26, No. 2. $21.95.
The Bering Sea, Vol. 26, No. 3. $21.95.
Russian America, Vol. 26, No. 4, $21.95.
Best of *ALASKA GEOGRAPHIC*®, Vol. 27, No. 1, $24.95.
Seals, Sea Lions and Sea Otters, Vol. 27, No. 2, $21.95.
Painting Alaska, Vol. 27, No. 3, $21.95.
Living Off the Land, Vol. 27, No. 4, $21.95.
Exploring Alaska's Birds, Vol. 28, No. 1, $23.95.
Glaciers of Alaska, Vol. 28, No. 2, $23.95.
Inupiaq and Yupik People of Alaska, Vol. 28, No. 3, $23.95.
The Iditarod, Vol. 28, No. 4, $23.95.
Secrets of the Aurora Borealis, Vol. 29, No. 1, $23.95.
Boating Alaska, Vol. 29, No. 2, $23.95.
Territory of Alaska, Vol. 29, No. 3, $23.95.
From Kodiak to Unalaska, Vol. 29, No. 4, $23.95.

* Available in hardback (library binding) — $24.95 each.

PRICES AND AVAILABILITY SUBJECT TO CHANGE

NEXT ISSUE: **Vol. 30, No. 2**

Juneau: Yesterday and Today

Discover Alaska's capital city in this all-new issue. Learn about Juneau's pioneers and the folks who thrive there today; the city's history as a gold-mining center; and modern pursuits such as fishing, tourism, and politics that make this such a dynamic place to live, work, and visit. To members summer 2003.